Instruction and Training for Enhanced Reference Service
Using Hands-on Active Learning Techniques

Vol. 2, pt. 2
Major Topics and their Reference Resources
Active Learning Series No. 3

Anne Cerstvik Nolan
and
Marilyn P. Whitmore,
Editors

Contributors:

Mary Ellen Collins
Katherine Furlong
Terri D. Hawkins
Audrey Abbott Iacone
John P. McDonough
Michael C. McGuire
Ann Perbohner
Gail M. Staines
Lawrence L. Tomikel
Thomas M. Twiss
Marilyn P. Whitmore

Library Instruction Publications

Permissions:
Permission is given individual librarians or classroom teachers to reproduce the exercises and handouts for classroom instruction and training. Reproductions of these materials for any other purpose is strictly prohibited without prior written permission of the publisher. The publisher may be contacted at 222 Lytton Avenue, Pittsburgh, PA 15213-1410.

Notice of Liability:
The information in this book is distributed on an "As is" basis, without warranty. While every precaution has been taken in the preparation of this book, neither the authors nor Library Instruction Publications shall have any liability to any person or entity with respect to any liability, loss, or damage caused or alleged to be caused directly or indirectly by the instructions or the accompanying disk component contained in this book.

Trademarks:
Several trademark names are used in this book. Rather than put a trademark symbol in the occurrences of the trademarked name, we are using the names only in an editorial fashion and to the benefit of the trademark owner, with no intention of infringement of the trademark.

Library of Congress Catalog Card Number: 98-066459
ISBN:0-9652711-4-5

Printed by Whitmore Printing & Typesetting in Lancaster, Pennsylvania

Table of Contents

Continuation of Volume 1

Introduction

This volume completes the three-part set entitled *Instruction and Training for Enhanced Reference Service Using Hands-on Active Learning Techniques*. The contents are as follows:

    Categories of Fact and Finding Reference Resources, Volume 1
    Reference Resources for the Disciplines, Volume 2, pt. 1
    Major Topics and their Reference Resources, Volume 2, pt. 2

Each chapter includes:
- an introduction to the topic,
- lesson plans (many of them in great detail),
- suggestions for preparing and presenting the topical material,
- lists of selected reference resources (all include a mix of print and electronic), and
- hands-on exercises specifically developed for the instruction session.

Hands-on exercises empower the trainee by providing immediate experience using both print and electronic resources to locate information. These are ready-made teaching materials to save the librarian many hours of preparation time.

All of the lesson plans are equally valuable and easily adapted for library instruction sessions; they are not meant to be used only for reference training. They are appropriate for upper-level high school classes, for junior college, for undergraduate college and university, for faculty groups, as well as other client groups in a public library setting.

The exercises, lists of reference resources, and any handouts are included on the disk that accompanies the book. Most chapters include only one or two examples of the exercises in the text; however, all of the exercises are on the disk. They may be customized to fit any individual library instruction and training needs.

The exercises are available in either Macintosh or DOS/Windows format; the software used is Microsoft WORD.

Librarians are invited to contact any of the contributing authors for additional information; each has included an e-mail address in the short biographies in the *Meet the Contributing Authors* section.

Anne Cerstvik Nolan and
Marilyn P. Whitmore, Editors

Meet the Contributing Authors

Mary Ellen Collins is an Associate Professor of Library Science and a Reference Librarian at the Purdue University Libraries. She taught in elementary school before joining the library profession. Since then, she has taught children's literature and reference in college and university settings, along with serving in libraries. Mary Ellen has also served on committees in ALA and state associations, and is the author of a book and several articles. Her MLS and PhD are from the University of Pittsburgh. E-mail:collinsm@sage.cc.purdue.edu

Katherine Furlong is the User Education and Electronic Resources Librarian at the University of Maine at Farmington. She received her BA in history and her MLIS from the University of Pittsburgh where she also worked as an intern at the Hillman Library reference desk. At UMF, Katherine provides reference service, coordinates the library's Information Literacy Program and maintains a 21-station electronic classroom. Her love of Shakespeare grew out of studies at the University of Sheffield, England, and volunteer work at the Folger Shakespeare Library in Washington, DC. Email—kfurlong@maine.maine.edu

Terri D. Hawkins is the Database Librarian at Sailor, Maryland's Online Public Information Network. Prior to this position, Terri spent five years at the Brown University Rockefeller Library in the Serials and Government Documents Departments. She holds a BA with honors in Anthropology from Brown University (1993) and an MS from Simmons College Graduate School of Library and Information Science (1997). E-mail—terri_hawkins@yahoo.com

Audrey Abbott Iacone is a Reference Librarian in the Pennsylvania Department of the Carnegie Library of Pittsburgh. Her areas of special interest include local history and genealogy. She has authored several articles, developed pathfinders on topics of local interest, and also designed a web site for locating information about regional orphanages—a topic of immense interest to genealogists and social historians. She teaches beginning genealogy classes and instructs library users on how to navigate genealogical web sites on the Internet. Audrey was an English major at Indiana University of Pennsylvania and received her MLS from the University of Pittsburgh. E-mail—iaconea@clpgh.org

John P. McDonough is a Library Information Specialist and Supervisor of Current Periodicals at the University of Pittsburgh's Hillman Library. John earned an MS in Environmental Science and Management in 1996 from Duquesne University. He has worked in environmental regulatory compliance but is hoping to find a position where he will be able to concentrate on the rehabilitation of injured animals. E-mail—jmcdon+@pitt.edu

Michael C. McGuire is the Head of Reference Services at the University of Maine at Farmington. He earned his AB at Colby College and the MLS from Syracuse University. A former cataloger, he now serves as coordinator and part of the teaching team for UMF's library instruction program. He also is the coordinator of the UMF Information Literacy Project, including several workshops held for the local service area.
E-mail—mmcguire@maine.maine.edu

Anne Cerstvik Nolan is Assistant Head, Reference Department at Brown University Library. She holds a BA in history from the University of Nevada-Reno and the MLS from Rutgers University. Anne is responsible for coordinating all reference training at Brown. Previously Anne was Acting Coordinator for Database Searching Services at the University of Pittsburgh. E-mail—Anne_Nolan@brown.edu

Ann Perbohner is Reference Librarian and Webmaster at the Health Sciences Libraries of Mercy Hospital of Pittsburgh. Ann has worked in automated services departments in both academic and public libraries. Her BA is from Shimer College and her MLIS from the University of Pittsburgh. E-mail—aperbohner@mercy.pmhs.org

Gail M. Staines is the Executive Director of the Western New York Library Resources Council in Buffalo, NY. Previously she was Coordinator of Information Education at Niagara County Community College, Sanborn, NY, for 10 years. Gail holds the MLS and PhD in Higher Education Administration from the University of Buffalo where she is also an adjunct Assistant Professor. Gail is a library instruction consultant and guest speaker and was selected to be on the first list of ACRL's Information Literacy Advisors. Gail is the author of numerous articles. E-mail—gstaines@wnylrc.org

Lawrence L. Tomikel holds a BA from California University of Pennsylvania and an MLS from the University of Pittsburgh. Larry has worked in the Reference Department of Hillman Library at the University of Pittsburgh for over 20 years. He has been a member of the Library School Interns Program teaching graduate students to work the Reference Desk since its inception in 1992. He is a member of the Library Instruction Working Group. E-mail—llt+@pitt.edu

Thomas M. Twiss is a Public Services Librarian at The College of New Jersey where his responsibilities include reference service, instruction, and electronic reference collection development. He holds an MS in LIS from Drexel University and an MA in Political Science from the University of Pittsburgh. He is the author of a number of publications dealing with Soviet politics and history. E-mail—twiss@tcnj.edu

Marilyn P. Whitmore is Editor of Library Instruction Publications and former Coordinator of Library Instruction in the University of Pittsburgh Libraries. She has been active in ALA, especially library instruction, collections development, and international library issues. Marilyn is the author of numerous publications. She holds the MLS from Rutgers University and PhD from the University of Pittsburgh. E-mail—mpw+@pitt.edu

Career and Job Hunting Resources

GAIL M. STAINES, PH.D.

Executive Director
WESTERN NEW YORK LIBRARY RESOURCES COUNCIL

Introduction

This chapter is designed to teach beginning reference librarians and library assistants how to search resources effectively for career-related information and job hunting information. Both print and electronic sources are included. Abstracts and indexes, reference books, periodicals, and Internet sites are the types of sources covered.

Components of the Instruction and Training

The instruction outlined in this chapter is progressive. Early activities involve teaching in a classroom environment. Students progress to individual self-learning activities working with an experienced reference librarian. Ideally, instruction would occur over the course of six weeks, with one instruction session or activity occurring each week.

A Listing of the Activities and Goals of the Activities

Activity 1—Learning about Career and Job Hunting Resources
>   Goal—To give trainees an overview of print and electronic sources which contain career and job hunting information and job vacancies.

Activity 2—Searching the Internet for Career and Job Information
>   Goal—To teach trainees how to effectively search the Internet for job-related and career helping information.

Activity 3—Job Hunting Resources: Testing Your Reference Skills
>   Goal—To have trainees test their knowledge and skill in locating information containing job vacancies.

Activity 4—Career and Job Hunting Resources: Print vs. Electronic
>   Goal—To have trainees compare and contrast the print and electronic versions of the *Occupational Outlook Handbook*.

Activity 5—Career and Job Hunting: Helping with Resumes and Interviewing
>   Goal—To have trainees test their knowledge and skill in locating resume and interviewing information.

Activity 6—Career and Job Hunting: Putting It All Together
>   Goal—To test student's knowledge and skill of locating career and job information using a variety of sources, both print and electronic.

Selected Career and Job Hunting Resources

Those sources available in electronic format (CD-ROM, Internet subscription) will be marked with a triple asterisk ***. In this chapter, the resources are listed in the following order:
Almanacs and Yearbooks
Directories
Guides and Handbooks
Indexes and Abstracts
Periodicals
Relevant Internet Sites

Almanacs and Yearbooks

The Almanac of International Jobs and Careers: A Guide to Over 1001 Employers. 1994 ed. This almanac provides readers with useful information on how to obtain employment in countries around the world. Areas covered include the U.S. Federal government, international organizations, corporations, consulting, nonprofit and voluntary organizations, higher education institutions, teaching overseas, and internship programs. Strategies on how to make employment contacts are also included. Entries provide address, phone, and fax numbers. An annotated bibliography of sources is included.

Directories

The Career Guide 1998: Dun & Bradstreet Employment Opportunities Directory, 1997. This is a directory of employers and career opportunities. It is arranged several ways including alphabetically by employer's name, geographically, by industry, branch offices geographically, and by discipline (geographically). Sections on employers with internship programs and a directory of personnel consultants are also included. This directory is targeted toward college graduates seeking employment. Entries include address and phone number of company, disciplines hired, brief company overview, company locations, and benefits packages.

The 1996 National Job Hotline Directory. 1996.
This resource provides listings of job opportunities available by phone; an 800-Toll Free listing of numbers is also included. It is organized alphabetically by state. Government, education, financial, medical, and miscellaneous categories are covered. It is indexed.

Guides and Handbooks

America's Top 300 Jobs, 1990–
Compiled from U.S. Dept. of Labor reports, this biennial reference source provides readers with information on job searching and changing careers. It is also useful for business owners and employers writing job descriptions and interviewing potential employees.

Exploring Tech Careers: Real People Tell You What You Need To Know. 1995.
This is an excellent source for those searching for information on technical-related careers. Information not only includes nature of the job, required education, salary, and

job outlook, but also interviews with people who work in the field. A list of professional organizations and a bibliography accompanies each entry.

Job Choices [series]
The National Association of Colleges and Employers publishes a series of career-related sources on a regular basis. Series titles include *Planning Job Choices: Four-Year College* edition, *Two-Year College* edition, and *Minorities* edition as well as *Job Choices in Science & Engineering*, and in *Business*. This series contains information on career planning, mentoring, future job forecasts, alternative careers, employment success, and company information.

Occupational Outlook Handbook, 1949– ***
This annual publication from the Bureau of Labor Statistics is considered the source for locating information about careers. For each career listing, the nature of the work involved, working conditions, employment, training required, job outlook, earnings, and related occupations are included. Additional sources to locate information are provided for each occupation. It is indexed by career and by *Dictionary of Occupational Title* number. The title is free on the Internet at—http://stats.bls.gov/ocohome.htm.

Specialty Occupational Outlook, 1994–
Gale Research enhances information found in the *Occupational Outlook Handbook* by highlighting an additional 150 job titles. There is a volume for *Professional* positions and another for *Trade and Technical* jobs. Both are useful for obtaining information on working conditions, education needed, salaries, related occupations, and bibliographies of more information.

Indexes and Abstracts
Searching abstracts and indexes for information on careers and job hunting will yield articles about resume writing and interviewing, and current/future "hot" jobs.

General indexes, such as *Expanded Academic Index*** or *Readers' Guide to Periodical Literature,*** will provide articles on general topics related to career and job hunting.

Searching subject specific indexes, such as *The Business Periodicals Index,*** *The Humanities Index,*** and *The Social Sciences Index,*** will retrieve articles related to careers and job hunting in specific topics covered by the index.

Periodicals
Major national and local newspapers, especially Sunday editions, are excellent places to locate employment opportunities. Some examples are:

Atlanta Journal - Atlanta Constitution	*St. Louis Dispatch*
Chicago Tribune	*Toronto Star*
Los Angeles Times	*Washington Post*
New York Times	

Trade and association periodicals are also excellent places to find employment opportunities. Check the reference title *Encyclopedia of Associations.* *** This will give you titles of publications published by profession-specific associations (e.g.: *American Libraries* published by the American Library Association) that usually contain job advertisements. Selected titles of professional journals are:

Advertising Age
American Artist
American Journal of Public Health
Animal Keeper's Forum
The Black Collegian
Broadcasting and Cable
Chronicle of Higher Education
Computer World
Corrections Today
Nurse Practitioner
Nursing
Police Career Digest
RN

Selected Major Subject Headings

Search the following subject headings for information about careers and job hunting:

Applications for positions	Job hotlines
Career changes	Job hunting
Civil service positions	Job vacancies
Employment agencies	Resumes (Employment)
Employment in foreign countries	Vocational guidance
Employment interviewing	

Relevant Internet Sites

The Internet can be very useful in helping with career planning and in locating job opportunities. Below is a brief list of Web sites you may want to consult.

America's Job Bank
http://www.ajb.dni.us
America's Job Bank is a partnership between the U.S. Department of Labor and the state operated public Employment Service. Job vacancies are primarily full-time, private sector positions; searches can be conducted by occupation. A geographic profile provides state demographic information. This site also provides a trends outlook for careers.

Career Mosaic
http://www.careermosaic.com/cm/cm1.html
This site contains a multitude of information on careers and job hunting. Search the J.O.B.S. database for position vacancies, post your resume for free, read resume writing tips in the Career Resource Center, check out the *CollegeConnection* for recent college graduates, or search the *International Gateway for Career Mosaic* sites worldwide.

Career Path
http://www.careerpath.com
Advertised as having "the Web's largest number of the most current job listings," *Career Path* gives you access to job postings in major U.S. newspapers and appearing in company Web sites. You can also post your resume and find information on employers in the Career section. Users may search several newspapers simultaneously.

Monster Board
http://www.monster.com
Search for jobs in the United States or internationally. Includes a Recruiters' Center, Career Center with resume builder, or let "Swoop" the Personal Job Search Agent search for positions for you for free.

Online Career Center
http://www.occ.com/occ
Use this site to search for company profiles and position openings by discipline and geographic location. Post your resume electronically. Relocation, immigration, and salary information also included.

The Riley Guide: Employment Opportunities and Job Resources on the Internet
http://www.dbm.com/jobguide
This site was created and maintained by Margaret F. Dikel (formerly Riley), author of several texts on job hunting. It is a great site to start a career search.

What Color Is Your Parachute: Job Hunting Online
http://www.washingtonpost.com/parachute
This is another outstanding site created and maintained by one of the leaders in the career and job searching field, Richard Nelson Bolles. It provides the user with a listing of vacancies, a place to post a resume and receive career counseling, to make contacts, find information and do career-related searching.

Hands-on Exercises

Below are several activities to use when you are instructing librarians and library staff how to search for information on job hunting. They have all been set up as worksheets and are included in this chapter; they are also on the accompanying disk. You may modify these exercises in any way to accommodate your training needs.

Activity 1—Learning About Career and Job Hunting Resources
> **Materials needed**: Reference books on careers and job hunting; Indexes (general and subject specific); Periodicals containing job vacancies (magazines, newspapers, professional journals

- Have trainees divide into groups of no more than 5 people.
- Give group one copies of reference books, group two copies of indexes (print and/or access to CD-ROM or via the Web), group three copies of periodicals. If there are

more than 3 groups, split sources by giving one group only magazines, one group newspapers, and one group professional journals.

- Ask each group to select one person to act as a recorder of notes for the group, one person to be the spokesperson, and one person to hold up the materials as they are being discussed.
- Provide each group with an "Answer These Questions—Finding Job Hunting & Career Information" handout. (See the end of this chapter for a copy you may duplicate.)
- Give the class 20 minutes to browse through their sources and answer the questions.
- After 20 minutes, have each group present answers to the questions. Allow 5 to 10 minutes for each group to present.
- Re-cap the discussion and findings at the end of the session.

Activity 2—Searching the Internet for Career and Job Information

The purpose of this activity is to teach library staff how to locate job hunting and career-related information using the Internet. It is assumed that participants have experience using a computer mouse, have worked in a Macintosh or Windows environment, and have familiarity with searching the World Wide Web for information.

Note: Instruction occurs in a computer lab classroom. Each trainee has his own computer. Trainees may be paired up to share a computer and work on this exercise.

- Provide trainees with a list of Internet sites such as those included in this chapter.
- Give each trainee or group of trainees, a specific site to search.
- Have trainees explore the site and take notes on the kinds of information available. Give trainees the handout "Exploring Internet and Career Sites" (which appears at the end of this chapter) and have them answer the questions. Give them 20 to 30 minutes to explore the site.
- Have each trainee or group of trainees explain to the whole class the purpose of the site and what kind of information can be located at the site. This is best done if the trainees stand in front of the class and bring up the site for the entire class to view on a screen.
- Re-cap the discussion and instruction at the end of the session.

Activity 3—Job Hunting Resources; Testing Your Reference Skills

Scenario: A patron comes to you looking for job vacancies for licensed practical nurses (LPN's) in the southeastern United States. The purpose of this exercise is for the trainee to become familiar with print and electronic sources, which provide information about job hunting and listings of job opportunities. The assignment is designed for an individual to work alone, then review the answers with an experienced reference librarian.

- Outline your strategy for helping this patron.
- What sources, print and electronic, would you refer him/her to?
- Conduct the search. Were you successful? Were there any sources you searched that did not yield information? What were the best sources to help this patron?

In reviewing your search strategy and actual search with an experienced reference librarian, is there anything you would do differently? Discuss it.

Actiivity 4—Career and Job Hunting Resources, Print vs. Electronic

The purpose of this exercise is to have the trainee compare information in print and electronic formats—*The Occupational Outlook Handbook* in print and electronic form. Once this exercise is completed, an experienced reference librarian should review it.

- Using the print version of *The Occupational Outlook Handbook*, locate information on becoming a veterinarian.
- Document the kind of information found? How long did the search take? Using the Internet, go to the *Occupational Outlook Handbook* Web site. Again, search for information on becoming a veterinarian. What kind of information was provided? How long did it take to search the Internet to locate this information? Was the information more current than the print version of the *Occupational Outlook Handbook?*
- The search should be reviewed with an experienced reference librarian. Advantages and disadvantages of using print and electronic sources to answer patrons' questions should be discussed.

Activity 5—Career and Job Hunting; Helping with Resumes and Interviews

Scenario: A patron asks you for help in locating books and articles on resume writing and how to interview. The patron also would like to know where he can post his resume for free on the Internet.

- The purpose of this assignment is to help trainees learn to help library patrons who ask for assistance in locating information on resume writing and interviewing skills. Once this activity, is completed, have an experienced reference librarian review the answers.
- Create a research strategy to help this patron. What are the best sources to search? What subject headings should be searched? Which Internet sites allow you to post your resume for free?
- Next the search should be conducted. It must be matched with the research strategy created. How successful was the search? What could be done differently?
- At the completion, the answers must be reviewed with an experienced reference librarian.

Activity 6—Career and Job Hunting; Putting It All Together

Now that the trainees have learned where and how to look for information on hunting for a job and searching for a career, let's put it all together. This exercise tests their knowledge and skill in locating job opportunities. Once completed, this assignment must be reviewed with an experienced reference librarian.

- Select a career, one that you are very interested in finding out more about.

- List the subject headings you are going to search under to find information on this career.
- Search your library's online catalog for books about this career. List two books.
- Search indexes, either print or electronic, for articles about this career. List citations to 2 articles.
- List several periodicals in this career area that provide job openings.
- Locate a professional association related to the career you selected. Search in the *Encyclopedia of Associations*. Write down the association's address and phone number.
- Search the Internet to see if the association has a Web site. What kind of information is available on this site? Can anyone view the information or is it only available to association members?
- Go to career and job related Web sites. (These are listed at the beginning of this chapter.)
- Search the career you selected on two of the sites. What kind of information did you locate? Which Web site yielded the most useful information?
- Review the assignment with an experienced reference librarian. If time and interest permits, consider creating a Webliography of the information you located.

Career and Job Hunting Exercise

Learning About Career and Job Hunting Resources

Your group has been given copies of reference resources and the handout "Answer These Questions—Finding Job Hunting & Career Information."

Step 1   Select one person to act as a recorder of notes for the group,

one person to be the spokesperson, and

one person to hold up the materials as they are being discussed.

Step 2   You will have 20 minutes to examine the resources and answer the questions on the handout.

Step 3   After 20 minutes, each group will make a presentation to the other groups. The presentation will be the answers to the questions on the handout. You will have no more than 10 minutes for the presentation.

Step 4   Be prepared to re-cap the discussion and findings at the end of the session.

NAME(S)...

Career and Job Hunting Exercise

Searching the Internet for Career and Job Information

The purpose of this activity is to learn how to locate job hunting and career-related information using the Internet. You will be working individually or with a partner.

Step 1   Each of you has been given a list of Internet sites to use for this exercise and a copy of the handout "Exploring Internet and Career Sites"

Step 2   Explore the sites; you will have 20 to 30 minutes to do this.

Take notes on the kinds of information available on the sites.

Answer the questions on the handout.

Step 3   At the end of the time, each individual or team, will explain to the whole class the purpose of the site and what kind of information can be located at the site.

Step 4   Be prepared to re-cap the discussion and instruction at the end of the session.

Career and Job Hunting Exercise

Job Hunting Resources—Testing Your Reference Skills

SCENARIO: A patron comes to you looking for job vacancies for licensed practical nurses (LPN's) in the southeastern United States.

The purpose of this exercise is for you to become familiar with print and electronic sources which provide information about job hunting and listings of job opportunities. The assignment is designed for you to work alone, then review your answers with an experienced reference librarian.

Part 1   Outline your strategy for helping this patron.

What sources, print and electronic, would you refer him/her to?

Part 2   Conduct the search. Were you successful? Were there any sources you searched that did not yield information? What were the best sources to help this patron?

Part 3   In reviewing your search strategy and actual search with an experienced reference librarian, is there anything you would do differently?

Discuss it here.

Career and Job Hunting Exercise

Career and Job Hunting Resources—Print vs. Electronic

The purpose of this exercise is to have you compare information in print and electronic formats. Specifically, you will be comparing **The Occupational Outlook Handbook** *in print and electronic form. Once you complete this exercise, have an experienced reference librarian review it with you.*

Step 1   Using the print version of *The Occupational Outlook Handbook*, locate information on becoming a veterinarian.

Document the kind of information did you found? How long did your search take you?

Step 2   Using the Internet, go to the *Occupational Outlook Handbook* Web site at: http://stats.bls.gov/ocohome.htm.

Again, search for information on becoming a veterinarian. What kind of information was provided? How long did you search the Internet to locate this information? Was the information more current than the print version of the *Occupational Outlook Handbook?*

Step 3   Review your search with an experienced reference librarian. Discuss the advantages and disadvantages of using print and electronic sources to answer patrons' questions.

Document your discussion.

Career and Job Hunting Exercise

Career and Job Hunting—Helping with Resumes and Interviews

SCENARIO: A patron asks you for help in locating books and articles on resume writing and how to interview. The patron also would like to know where he can post his resume for free on the Internet.

The purpose of this assignment is to help you learn to help library patrons who ask for assistance in locating information on resume writing and interviewing skills. Once you complete this activity, have an experienced reference librarian review your answers.

Part 1   Create a research strategy to help this patron.

What are the best sources to search?

What subject headings should be searched?

Which Internet sites allow you to post your resume for free?

Part 2   Conduct your search. Match your search with the research strategy you created
         in Part 1.

         How successful were you in your search?

         What would you do differently?

Part 3   Review your answers with an experienced reference librarian.

Career and Job Hunting Exercise

Career and Job Hunting—Putting It All Together

Now that you have learned where and how to look for information on hunting for a job and searching for a career, let's put it all together. This exercise tests your knowledge and skill in locating job opportunities. Once completed, review this assignment with an experienced reference librarian.

Step 1   Select a career, one that you are very interested in finding out more about. Complete the worksheet below.

Career you selected: _____

Step 2   List the subject headings you are going to search under to find information on this career.

Step 3   Search your library's online catalog for books about this career. List two books:

Author(s): _____

Title: _____

Publisher: _____

Place of publication: _____

Date: _____

Author(s): _____

Title: _____

Publisher: _____

Place of publication: _____

Date: _____

Step 4   Search indexes, either print or electronic, for articles about this career.

List citations to 2 articles you found:

Author(s): _____

Article title: _____

Periodical title: _____

Date of issue: _____

Volume & number (if given): _____

Pages: _____

Author(s): _____

Article title: _____

Periodical title: _____

Date of issue: _____

Volume & number (if given): _____

Pages: _____

Step 5   List several periodicals in this career area that provide job openings:

Step 6   Locate a professional association related to the career you selected. Search in the *Encyclopedia of Associations*. Write down the association's address and phone number:

Step 7   Search the Internet to see if the association has a Web site.

What kind of information is available on this site? Can anyone view the information or is it only available to association members?

Step 8   Go to career and job related Web sites. (These are listed at the beginning of this chapter.)

Search the career you selected on two of the sites. What kind of information did you locate? Which Web site yielded the most useful information?

Step 9   Review the assignment with an experienced reference librarian. If time and interest permits, consider creating a Webliography of the information you located.

ANSWER THESE QUESTIONS:

FINDING JOB HUNTING AND CAREER INFORMATION

Examine the sources you have been given and answer the questions below.

1.   What is the exact title of your source?

2.   Who is the author(s)?

3.   How often is the source published? Updated?

4.   What is the date of publication listed on your source?

5.   What kind of information does this source provide?

6.   Is this source a part of a series, or can it stand alone as its own source?

7.   How would this source be useful to people looking for job hunting and career information?

EXPLORING INTERNET CAREER AND JOB SITES

This worksheet is designed for instruction outlined in Activity Two in this chapter. Working alone or in pairs, search a Web site that provides job and career-related information and answer the questions below.

No. 1   What site did you search? Give the name of the site and the URL address.

Name of site: _____

URL address: http:// _____

No. 2   When was this site last updated? _____

No. 3   Who (what person) is responsible for creating and maintaining the information on this Web site? _____

No. 4   What are this person's credentials? (MD, Ph.D., MLS, etc.) _____

No. 5   With what institution (college, university, organization, company, etc.) is this site associated?

No. 6   What kind of information is provided at this site? (Check all that apply.)

_____Job postings (If yes, are they local, national, and/or international?)

_____Background information on careers

_____Information on resume writing

_____Information on interviewing

_____A place to post your resume (Is there any cost involved?)

_____Other: _____

No. 7   Search the Web site by looking under a career/job of your choice.

What career did you search for? _____

What kind of information did you retrieve? _____

_____

No. 8   How would this Web site be useful to people looking for job related information?

Consumer Health Information

ANN PERBOHNER

Reference Librarian, Webmaster
MERCY HOSPITAL LIBRARY, PITTSBURGH

Introduction

- "I just heard about a new drug for asthma and need more information before talking with my doctor."
- "Does Kava Kava really work for insomnia and are there any side effects?"

With the explosion of access to health information and the public's interest in medical self-care, librarians are faced with health related questions from patients and consumers with increasing frequency. These types of questions are often challenging for librarians, especially those not trained in providing medical information to consumers.

"Consumer health information (CHI) is information on health and medical topics provided in response to requests from the general public, including patients and their families. In addition to information on the symptoms, diagnosis, and treatment of disease, CHI encompasses information on health promotion, preventive medicine, the determinants of health, and accessing the health care system." (From Policy Statement by the Medical Library Association and the Consumer and Patient Health Information Section (CAPHIS/MLA). "The Librarian's Role in the Provision of Consumer Health Information and Patient Education." *Bulletin of the Medical Library Association 84* (April 1996):238–239.

Components of the Instruction and Training

- Determine what librarians need to know in order to provide CHI in your library.
- Consider your instructional objectives and write them down.
- Develop written handouts to support training and delivery of CHI. This is a good opportunity to develop a mission statement for CHI or a disclaimer statement to give your library patrons.
- Consider developing a handout of local health resources and support groups.
- Select resources from your reference and circulating collections to answer some of the instructional problems discussed in your presentation.
- Use this as an opportunity to familiarize your staff with your medical and CHI collection.
- Pre-select and bookmark Internet sites to demonstrate using the Internet for CHI.
- Encourage the participants to complete the exercises on their own. Allow them time to discuss their answers and approach to questions during the training session.

Guidelines for Consumer Health Information Reference Service

While librarians are not practicing health professionals, they may play an active role in providing health information. Librarians need to be careful not to interpret information or give advice to clients. If they do, they are stepping over the boundary of practicing medicine and may be putting themselves at risk legally. Clear guidelines must therefore be set for the provision of a CHI service. This may include developing a service policy and ensuring that it is explained to patrons in a sensitive way. This chapter discusses aspects of the reference interview and delivery of service. For a complete overview of setting up a CHI service, consult *Developing a Consumer Health Information Service: A Practical Guide* (1995) by Susan Murray of the Metropolitan Toronto Reference Library.

Some of the reference issues encountered with CHI are different than those which concern less personal reference questions. Many of your clients may feel particularly vulnerable or anxious. You may be uncomfortable with the personal nature of CHI. Other aspects of CHI include the following:

- Clients have varying literacy levels requiring different sources or types of information. Some clients may prefer lay literature while others prefer professional materials.
- Librarians may have discomfort providing unfavorable information.
- The consumer may have expectations that they will find an answer to their problem or that the librarian will interpret medical information.
- Sometimes there is too little or too much information on some topics.

Recognize your role as a librarian and your limitations in providing information. The best recourse may be to refer your client to someone else.

A complete handout of guidelines for a CHI reference service that can be used for discussion during your training session follows. Permission to include these **Guidelines for Providing Medical Information to Consumers** is courtesy of "Healthnet: Connecticut Consumer Health Information Network, Lyman Maynard Stowe Library, University of Connecticut Health Center, Farmington CT."

Guidelines for Providing Medical Information to Consumers

The following are suggested guidelines for providing medical information to consumers. These questions are those that relate directly to a personal medical concern of the person asking for information or the person's relative or friend. Consumer questions, within the context of these guidelines, **do not** include questions from students doing research for a school report, health professionals, or someone doing work-related research.

1. **Determine why the person needs the information**
   Health reference questions differ from most general reference questions because they often deal with sensitive information. Also, when assisting someone who has a health question, it's important to make the distinction between questions related to a

personal health concern and those related to a school project or work. Often someone with a personal health question requires very specific information, whereas someone writing a school report may want a broad overview of the topic.

If you feel uncomfortable about asking the person why he needs the information or the topic is of a sensitive nature, consider asking "Do you need this information for a school report or for your work?" If the person responds "No," assume the question is of a personal nature. In most instances, the person will not hesitate to relate the reason they need the information.

2. **Be aware of the person who is asking the question**
   The typical consumer health question comes from someone who has just been diagnosed or has just learned that a family member is ill. The person may be upset and may not be clear about the information he needs.

   Remember that the person you are speaking to may not be the person in question. Parents, other family members, or friends may be asking for the information, so be sure to determine the age and sex of the person in question. Often a disease may affect a child differently than an adult and treatments can vary depending upon a person's age and sex.

3. **Get as much information as possible**
   Ask open-ended questions to get as much information about what the person specifically wants to know. Most people will freely discuss their medical concern, but there are times when someone may be reluctant to do so because of the nature of the question. You may want to consider saying; "It will help me find the information you need if you can tell me more about what you want to know."

   Also you can save a great deal of time by determining what the person already knows about the subject. Has the person already consulted sources in your library and, if so, which ones? Was the information found not satisfactory and, if so, why? Was it too technical? Too general? Not current enough?

   Avoid putting words in the person's mouth. If she isn't sure about the correct terminology, try not to offer suggestions. If you offer a specific phrase or term, the person may agree that what you are saying is what she wants, even when it is not.

   Try to get an idea of how much and what kind of information the person wants. If the question is about a disease consider asking "Are you looking for a general overview or do you want something more specific?" If the person responds that he wants all information available, try to get him to be more specific. It would be impossible, for example, to provide all the available information about arthritis since there is so much published about this disease.

4. **Never assume you know what the person wants to know**

    Some people will readily tell you everything they want to know and be clear and specific with their questions. Others may be uncertain about the information they want. Do not assume you know what information may be important to the person. If you had a similar question in the past, you may be tempted to think that this person wants the same information.

5. **Always check terms in a medical dictionary**

    Always check in a medical dictionary for unfamiliar terms **before** you begin to help the person with a question. If he is uncertain about the spelling of a medical term and you are also uncertain, check variants of spelling but don't go too far afield. If you have done a thorough search and still cannot find the term, suggest that the person get the correct terminology and spelling from his doctor.

    If the person is uncertain about the spelling of a drug name, variants **should not** be checked as this could lead to inaccurate information. Many drugs have similar sounding names but are prescribed for very different reasons. Ask the person to get the correct spelling of the drug name from his physician or pharmacist before attempting to answer the question.

6. **Do not provide a diagnosis**

    A person may ask a health question by reciting a variety of symptoms and expect you to provide a diagnosis. He isn't exactly sure what his doctor said and he is reluctant to call her for the specific diagnosis. You may know the answer because your aunt has the same condition, but do not provide a diagnosis (even if the person is well known to library staff or is a friend). The person who persists in seeking a diagnosis can be referred to the *AMA Family Medical Guide* which has a 200 page section with self-diagnosis symptom charts. These charts guide the reader through different questions and recommend a course of action for specific symptoms.

7. **Do not interpret medical information**

    Medical information is often very technical. If the person asks you the meaning of a specific term or sentence, refrain from saying what you "think" the information means (even if you are absolutely certain). Suggest that the person consult a medical dictionary or the *AMA Encyclopedia of Medicine* for definitions of technical terms.

8. **Do not give medical advice, opinions, or make recommendations**

    You may be assisting a person find information and they may ask you questions such as "Do you think I should…get a second opinion…try a different medication…etc." or "What's the best…clinic…treatment…etc?" It's difficult not to answer the person's concerns, especially if you know the person. Be very clear, however, that you cannot provide an opinion and that you have no medical training as a doctor. Suggest that you will be happy to search further if the person requires additional information. If the person is persistent about wanting advice or recommendations, suggest that she discuss this with her physician.

NEVER provide a recommendation for a specific physician even if you are convinced that your surgeon, pediatrician, etc. is the best in the world. If the person wants a recommendation, suggest that she call a local hospital. Many hospitals have physician referral services. These referral services, however, do not give information about a physician's competence -- they only provide 3 or 4 names of physicians who have privileges at that particular hospital.

You may also suggest that the person check a physician's qualifications by consulting the *ABMS Compendium of Certified Medical Specialists* or the *Directory of Physicians in the United States*. These sources only give background information on physicians; they do not rate them. You can also check resources such as *The Best Doctors in America* which is a listing of doctors recommended by other doctors as being experts in their field. Another resource to consider is the medical society in your state. Self-help groups with the same medical concern as the person may also be a source of information on specific physicians.

9. **Understand that the specific information the person wants may not be available anywhere in the medical literature and describe the limitations of medical information**

   People who have questions about a personal health concern may expect to find information directly related to their own unique medical conditions in language he can understand. They often want to find straightforward answers to complex questions so they can make clear-cut decisions about a medical problem. Also, many do not understand that the medical literature often does not reflect a consensus on various treatment options for a specific disease.

   The person may have to be satisfied with an incomplete answer to her question. Be aware, however, that the effective reference interview may result in a reformulation of the original request which may yield a great deal of information. Often the reformulated question is what the person wanted to ask in the first place.

   If appropriate, explain to the person the limitations of medical information. You may explain that information becomes quickly outdated, that medical experts often disagree about the diagnosis and treatment of a specific disease, and that the majority of medical information is written in technical language.

10. **Provide the most complete information needed to answer the person's specific request**

    This is the ultimate goal of all reference work. Certain medical questions, however, can present unique problems. A person may have a question about the diagnosis, treatment, and prognosis of a specific disease that you know or later find out is usually fatal. What should you do? If the person has telephoned the library and you are uncomfortable about discussing the information over the phone, offer to make a photocopy to mail to the person. You should never under any circumstance, withhold information since this can be considered a form of censorship. Often a person who wants information about a serious disease may already suspect the prognosis.

11. **Consider referring persons to self-help groups or health organizations for certain kinds of information**

If a person is looking for a recommendation for a physician who treats a specific disease or medical condition, consider referring the person to a self-help group whose members have the same medical concern. Self-help group members often share information about specific physicians they've found to be most helpful in treating their condition. Many may know about all the latest options (conventional and alternative) and the support services available in the community. Be clear, however, that you are recommending a self-help group as an information resource, lest he think you are suggesting he needs emotional support to cope with his problem consult *The Self-help Directory: A Guide to Connecticut and National Groups* for a listing of these groups. If the *Directory* doesn't list a specific group, call (or suggest the person call) the Connecticut Self-help network to see if there is more current information on a group. The Network's telephone number is (203) 624-6982 (New Haven).

Associations concerned with a specific disease or medical condition often have up-to-date information on the latest research and treatments. Some also has a medical advisor on their staff who will talk with the person in need of the information. Often associations publish newsletters or issue bulletins with information on new treatments. Check the *Encyclopedia of Associations* or the *Self-help Directory* for the names of these organizations and associations.

12. **Consider referring cancer related questions to the National Cancer Institute's Cancer Information Service 1-800-CANCER**

The National Cancer Institute maintains a free telephone information service for cancer patients and their families. Trained professionals will answer the caller's questions either over the phone or, more likely, by conducting a search of the information services database called *Physician's Data Query (PDQ)*. The information from this database, plus other printed literature, will be sent to the caller.

Libraries with Internet access may want to consider using *Oncolink* at (http://cancer.med.upenn.edu). The *Oncolink* offers access to the *PDQ* database of information on cancer treatments, and other important cancer information, such as current news stories related to cancer, self-help groups, clinical trials, and patient education materials.

Selected Consumer Health Reference Resources

The resources selected for inclusion in this chapter are a sampling of those that have been published. Those sources that are also in electronic format (CD-ROM, Internet subscription) will be marked with a triple asterisk ***. The resources are arranged in the following categories:
   Selecting Consumer Health Information
   Indexes and Databases
   Dictionaries and Encyclopedias
   Directories
   Handbooks and Manuals
   Journals
   Newsletters
   Pamphlet series
   Additional relevant Internet sites

See also the chapter "Medical Sciences" by Brittney G. Chenault in *Instruction and Training for Enhanced Reference Service,* v.2, pt.1, p. 151–179.

Selecting Consumer Health Information

Consumer Health Information Source Book. 1997 ed.
Use this book for locating clearinghouses, hotlines, books, magazines, electronic, and Internet resources. The *Consumer Health Information Source Book* is the classic print resource for locating and accessing CHI. This book is also available as part of the IAC™ CD-ROM Health Reference Center.

The Consumer Health Bibliography for the Small Public Library, January, 1998.
http://www.njc.org/caphis/ConsHealthBib.html
The Consumer and Patient Health Information Section (CAPHIS) of the Medical Library Association provides a basic bibliography of 37 titles to begin a CHI collection. The CAPHIS web site includes other resources for CHI librarians.

Core Bibliography of Consumer Health Reference Books, February, 1999.
http://www3.uchc.edu/~uchclib/departm/hnet/corelist.html
The Lyman Maynard Stowe Library of the University of Connecticut Health Center at Farmington, lists recommended titles for public library CHI questions. This list of 76 titles is arranged in 20 categories. Core titles are suggested for any library collection, and additional titles are recommended for large libraries or comprehensive collections. *Healthnet News*, a newsletter for librarians and others interested in CHI, is also available on this site.

EBSCO
http://www.ebsco.com
Published on a yearly basis, *EBSCO Journals in Consumer Health* includes titles, ISSN, price, and publisher information. Alternative medicine titles are included.

Majors Scientific Books, Inc.
http://www.majors.com
Majors is a book distributor whose printed book lists include Complementary Health, Consumer Health, and Women's Health. The Consumer Health catalog indicates titles in the *Consumer Health Information Source Book.*

Indexes and Databases for Consumer Health Information

Consumer Health & Nutrition Index, 1985–
This index includes over 70 popular health letters, medical journals, magazines, and other selected articles from *The New York Times* and *The Wall Street Journal.*

CINAHL, Cumulative Index to Nursing and Allied Health Literature, 1982–
This title is available in print, on CD-ROM, and on the Internet—http://www.cinahl.com. Approximately 650 journals are indexed from 1982. A recent addition to *CINAHL* is a journal subset containing over 50 consumer health titles.

Health Reference Center (HRC)
http://library.iacnet.com/html/hrc.html
The *HRC* from the Information Access Company includes access to 110 full text publications, 500 pamphlets, and six reference titles. The titles are:
Mosby's Medical, Nursing and Allied Health Dictionary
Columbia University College of Physicians and Surgeons Complete Home Medical Guide; People's Book of Medical Tests
USP DI: Advice for the Patient, Drug Information in Lay Language
The Consumer Health Information Source Book, and
The Complete Directory for People with Chronic Illness

Health Source Plus
http://www.ebsco.com
Health Source Plus from EBSCO Publishing contains over 1,000 pamphlets and abstracts and indexing for 500 consumer health, nutrition, and professional journals. Over 200 periodicals are provided full text.

Medline
Issued by the National Library of Medicine, *Medline* indexes over 3,900 journals including the premier medical journals and a few selected consumer health and complementary medicine titles. While *Medline* can be used for consumer health and nutrition topics, most of the indexed articles are of a highly technical nature and are not suitable for consumer health reference. The *Abridged Index Medicus* (*ABM*) is no longer in print, but the key professional journals which comprise the *ABM* can still be selected as one of the journal subsets in some editions of *Medline.* The National Library of Medicine provides free access to *Medline* through *PubMed* at— http://www.ncbi.nlm.nih.gov/PubMed/.

Northern Light

http://www.nlsearch.com

For those without access to print or online indexes, *Northern Light* is a resource for any research topic, including consumer health. *Northern Light* is an Internet search engine as well as a search utility for 5,000 journals and other titles in print. For a small fee, articles may be purchased online for immediate printing.

Dictionaries and Encyclopedias

Dictionary of Medical Syndromes. 1997 ed.
A dictionary of syndromes is a good supplement to other dictionaries in your collection. This revised edition includes 200 new syndromes and an index of synonyms.

Miller-Keane Encyclopedia & Dictionary of Medicine, Nursing & Allied Health. 1997.
Written for the allied health or nursing professional, this dictionary is easier for the consumer to understand than Stedman's.

Stedman's Medical Dictionary. 1995 ed.
Every collection should have at least one authoritative medical dictionary. Stedman's is a good choice to include in any medical collection.

Directories

The Best Doctors in America. 1996–1997 ed. (biennial)
Published in U.S. regional editions, *Best Doctors...* includes names, specialization, and affiliations for the selected physicians.

The Best Hospitals in America. 1995.
This popular book can help your patrons choose a specialized care facility. The book is organized regionally and hospital entries include research done and programs for each facility.

Handbooks and Manuals

General Handbooks and Manuals

Complete Guide to Symptoms, Illness and Surgery. 1995 ed.
This title covers over 2,000 symptoms, 500 illnesses, and 170 surgeries. Written for the patient, this book explains such questions as what will happen, and why, or what to expect.

Current Medical Diagnosis and Treatment, 1974–   (annual)
Although this publication is written for a professional audience, it is a good first choice for understanding the diagnosis and treatment of many diseases.

Harrison's Principles of Internal Medicine. 1998 ed. ***
Written for professionals, Harrison's offers detailed information that adds to information not covered in consumer oriented books. A CD-ROM version is available.

Mayo Clinic Family Health Book. 1996. ***
This comprehensive guide, written for the consumer, covers diseases and disorders. A CD-ROM version is also available.

Merck Manual of Medical Information: Home Edition. 1997.
Originally written as a professional manual, this is the consumer edition of a popular reference work.

Physicians' Guide to Rare Diseases. 1995 ed.
Written for physicians, this guide is easily understood by the medical consumer. Features include a color atlas of visual signs and references to orphan drugs.

Topical Handbooks and Manuals
Aging
Merck Manual of Geriatrics. 1999 ed.
Nutrition, falls, and sleep disorders are among the topics in the newest edition of the *Merck Manual of Geriatrics.* The 1995 edition is online at—http://www.merck.com.

AIDS
Home Care Guide for HIV and AIDS: For Family and Friends Giving Care at Home. 1997.
This is a well-organized how-to book for assisting with the daily needs of people living with AIDS. It is part of the Home Care Guides series from the American College of Physicians.

Alternative Complementary Medicine
The Encyclopedia of Natural Medicine. 1997.
Written by naturopathic doctors, this book combines a look at scientific evidence with a natural approach to prevention and treatment of disease.

PDR for Herbal Medicines. 1998.
Based on the work of the German Commission E, the *PDR for Herbal Medicines* includes pharmacological effects, interactions, and contraindications for herbal remedies.

Anatomy
The Human Body: An Illustrated Guide to Its Structure, Function, & Disorders. 1995.
This atlas uses color photographs and computer generated images to illustrate the human body and its organs.

Cancer

Informed Decisions: The Complete Book of Cancer Diagnosis, Treatment and Recovery.
1997.
This volume from American Cancer Society Staff covers cancer detection through
recovery.

Diabetes
Diabetes: The Complete Guide a Massachusetts General Hospital Book. 1997.
This is an authoritative and up-to-date guide to managing diabetes.

Drug Handbooks
Physicians' Desk Reference, 1974– (annual)
Known as the *PDR,* this is the drug handbook your clients may ask for, but it is not as
easy to understand as the *USP DI: Advice for the Patient, Drug Information in Lay
Language.*

USP DI: Advice for the Patient, Drug Information in Lay Language, 1983– (annual)
This is the U.S. Pharmacopeial Convention annual. Written for the public, this volume
covers prescription and non-prescription medications.

Heart Disease
Heart Disease: A Textbook of Cardiovascular Medicine. 1996 ed.
Heart Disease... is a comprehensive professional textbook for in-depth reference that is
also easy to understand.

Mayo Clinic Heart Book. 1993.
A highly recommended book on cardiovascular health that is published for the consumer
population.

Mental Health
Caring for the Mind: The Comprehensive Guide to Mental Health. 1996.
This book offers clear descriptions on mental health and mental disorders for the lay
public.

Nutrition
Nutrition Almanac. 1996 ed.
This expanded and updated edition covers nutrients, ailments, herbs, and more.

Nutrition Facts Manual: A Quick Reference. 1996.
With its tabular format, the *Nutrition Facts Manual* works well as a ready-reference
resource.

Pediatrics

American Medical Association Complete Guide to Your Children's Health. 1999.
From A to Z, more than 300 childhood diseases and disorders are discussed. Illustrated
with photographs and charts, this book, published by the American Medical Association,
has chapters that cover from infancy through adolescence.

Nelson Textbook of Pediatrcs. 1999.
Nelson Textbook of Pediatrics is a professional reference for detailed pediatric diagnosis
and treatment information.

Surgery
Current Surgical Diagnosis and Treatment. 1999.
This title covers, in a concise manner, aspects of surgery from inpatient to outpatient and
ambulatory care.

Tests
The Patient's Guide to Medical Tests. 1997.
Written by faculty from Yale University School of Medicine, this guide to medical tests
is easy to understand for the average consumer.

Women's Health
Our Bodies, Ourselves for the New Century: A Book by & for Women. 1998 ed.
Updated again, this popular book covers women's health and sexuality. New issues are
examined such as lesbians having children and racism and its effect on women's health.

Journals

The following journals are either frequently cited in the news, or contain medical articles
that are easy to understand.

American Family Physician ***
http://www.aafp.org
The *American Family Physician,* in print and online, includes patient education handouts
that can be used as reference material. It is published by the American Academy of
Family Physicians.

JAMA: The Journal of the American Medical Association ***
http://www.ama-assn.org/public/journals/jama/
JAMA includes "Patient Pages" in the back of each issue that are designed as patient
education handouts. "Patient Pages" are also available on the Internet site.

New England Journal of Medicine ***
http://www.nejm.org
This title from the Massachusetts Medical Society is one of the most respected.

Patient Care ***

http://www.pdr.net/pcmag/

Online versions of patient education handouts can be found on the *Patient Care* Internet site.

Newsletters

Harvard Medical School was the first major medical institution to publish a consumer health newsletter 25 years ago, *The Harvard Health Letter*. *The Health Letter* continues to be published along with the *Heart Letter, Mental Health Letter, Women's Health Watch*, and the newest publication *Men's Health Watch*. These are all well written and popular information resources from—http://www.harvardhealthpubs.org/—Harvard Health Publications, 164 Longwood Avenue, Boston, MA 02115.

Pamphlet series

Well-Connected Series
http://www.well-connected.com/
This reasonably priced series of up-to-date information is prepared and edited by physicians at Harvard Medical School. A complete set containing over 90 topics sells for $250 including photocopy rights. Report topics include depression, impotence, skin wrinkles, etc. Sample topics can be found on the *NOAH* Internet site at—
http://www.noah.cuny.edu/providers/wellconn.html.

Additional Relevant Internet Sites

Comprehensive sites

The Consumer Health Information Service at the Toronto Reference Library
http://www.mtrl.toronto.on.ca/centres/chis/urls98.htm
The links to consumer health Internet sites are well selected so you have only a few choices per category.

Health On the Net (HON)
http://www.hon.ch/MedHunt/
HON is a medical search engine containing only evaluated Web sites that meet specific quality criteria.

Healthfinder
http://www.healthfinder.gov
This site is sponsored by the U.S. Department of Human Services. From prevention to diagnosis and treatments, *Healthfinder* sites are chosen for their clarity and authority for the consumer.

New York Online Access to Health (NOAH)
http://www.noah.cuny.edu/

Bilingual in English and Spanish, *NOAH* provides high quality, full text material for consumers.

Topical Sites

Cancer

Oncolink
http://www.oncolink.com
This is an award winning site with disease oriented information categorized by cancer type. Topics include support information, cancer causes, screening and prevention, resources for patients and clinical trials.

Children's Health

Children's health
http://kidshealth.org
Climb aboard to the site organized by client groups: parents, teens, and kids.

Clinical Trials

Clinical trials
http://www.centerwatch.com/
This is a searchable listing of clinical trials by disease category.

Disabilities

Disability
http://www.disabilityresources.org
This guide to disability resources on the web includes disabilities by subject and regional resources.

Family Medicine

Family Medicine
http://cpmcnet.columbia.edu/texts/guide/
The Columbia University College of Physicians and Surgeons Complete Home Medical Guide is online. It includes chapters on nutrition, adolescence and men's health.

Journals

MedWebpPlus
http:// http://www.medwebplus.com/subject/Periodicals.html
Many medical journals have Internet sites containing table of contents or full text articles. *MedWebpPlus* is a good source for locating these online journals.

Low Literacy

LSU Medical Center
http://lib-sh.lsumc.edu/fammed/pted/pted.html
Designed for use by physicians and health educators, these resources from Louisiana State University Medical Center include low literacy documents organized into 15 specialty areas.

U.S. Food and Drug Agency
http://www.fda.gov/opacom/lowlit/7lowlit.html
These are easy-to-read brochures from the Food and Drug Administration and are in English and Spanish.

Mental Health

Mental Health Net
http://www.cmhc.com
This site covers disorders and treatment for consumers as well as professionals.

Medline for Consumers

MedlinePlus
http://medlineplus.nlm.nih.gov/medlineplus/
Easier to use than *PubMed*, *MedlinePlus* guides consumers through filtered searches.

Self-Help Groups

Self-Help Sourcebook Online
http://mentalhelp.net/selfhelp/
This is the American Self-help Clearinghouse *Self-Help Sourcebook Online*.

Hands-on Exercises

These training exercises are designed to help familiarize training participants with locating CHI in your library. Library policies vary concerning the level of assistance given to consumers with health questions. Some library policies direct the librarian to assist the client in using the materials, but not to select a specific book or resource for the client. Other library policies call for the librarian to help with the selection of resources, based on the needs and requests of the client. Consult your library policies for further guidance on this issue.

Two exercises, with all steps, are included in the text at the end of the chapter. The remaining exercises will be found only on the accompanying disk. All of the exercises may be customized to fit the circumstances in individual libraries.

- A young woman comes to your desk and asks, "Where can I find out about lowering my cholesterol levels without taking medication?"

- A patron has become very upset discussing the diagnosis of Alzheimer's disease in his father.

- A patron asks to see a copy of Derek Humphrey's book *Final Exit*.

- A patron approaches you and says, "I'm looking for breast cancer treatment information. I am interested in both alternative and western medical treatments."

- Locate information resources from your collection and on the Internet which can answer the following questions:
  Does Kava Kava really work for insomnia?
  How much should I take?
  Are there any side effects using Kava Kava?
  What are the contraindications in taking Kava Kava?

Consumer Health Exercise

A young woman comes to your desk and asks, "Where can I find out about lowering my cholesterol levels without taking medication?"

Complete the steps listed below and list the answer to the topic question.

Step 1   Select a print resource from your collection to fill this information need.

        Resource:

Step 2   Which Internet site would you choose and why?

Step 3   Which online resource would you choose if the patron asks for something easy to read?

Step 4   Which online resource would you choose if the patron was highly educated, or a
          health professional and why?

Consumer Health Exercise

A patron has become very upset discussing the diagnosis of Alzheimer's disease in his father.

Complete the steps listed below and list the answer to the topic question.

Step 1   How do you handle the situation? Discuss your strategy.

Step 2   Which of your print reference items do you point your clients to and why? List the resources.

Step 3   What do you say when the patron asks you which treatment or provider you would use? Discuss this.

Notes:

Debate or Argument Resources

MARILYN P. WHITMORE, PH.D.

Editor
LIBRARY INSTRUCTION PUBLICATIONS

Introduction

"Debate is one of the oldest activities of civilization. Calm, orderly debate, in which speakers ague for acceptance of various answers to a given question, is an obvious feature of modern parliaments and congresses. But it also had its place in the deliberations of ancient kings, who maintained councils of nobles to give them advice. When the nobles disagreed, they were allowed to debate their proposals before the king, who acted as the final judge in choosing one plan of action."—*Ericson and Murphy* (*The Debater's Guide* by Jon M. Ericson & James J. Murphy, with Raymond Bud Zeuschner. Carbondale: Southern Illinois University Press, Rev. ed., c1987)

Effective speakers can convince people on behalf of their solution to a problem. For example, proponents can speak on behalf of a proposal and convince enough people to vote for it in an upcoming election. On the other hand, a good speaker can oppose the proposal by a skillful defense of the present system. Formal debating is done by members of legislative bodies and the same basic principles are involved. Intercollegiate debate has taken place since 1892 when Harvard and Yale participated in an academic debate. And still today millions of American high school and college students participate in school debating.

"Actually, every situation which asks you to compare alternatives is a situation forcing you to debate the merits of those alternatives. Sometimes you will be debating within yourself, as when you must decide where to attend college. Sometimes the debating is done in your presence by others, with you as the judge, as in the case of rival sales representatives, each of whom asks you to buy his or her particular product."—*Ericson and Murphy*

Student debating can be a useful and meaningful experience because throughout life one encounters situations that challenge us to communicate effectively on important issues, especially public issues. "Debate skill cannot by itself make good citizens, but the American who cannot speak effectively in an organized way is a voiceless citizen, one whose good ideas may be lost in the crowd or never heard. Debating, consequently can be highly valuable both to you and to your society."—*Ericson and Murphy*

What is Necessary To Begin?

Students enrolled in debating and public speaking classes will have to prepare persuasive speeches. And in many other classes, students are required to write argumentative papers on some contemporary issue. Students who are under the tutelage of a professor most likely will have been given a strategy or guidelines or an outline of how to begin to collect and organize ideas for the debate or paper. Debate texts generally include a chapter on how to research a topic.

Debate Proposition

First of all, the debaters have to make a proposition for debate. For example, capital punishment should be abolished. In this case, "capital punishment" is the subject and "should be abolished" is what is proposed. It is only through library research of the proposition that debaters can attempt a successful debate.

Debate Research—Background Reading

Students often choose to investigate topics about which they know little. Therefore, they only have one option and that is to familiarize themselves with as much relevant information as they can. Debate research should begin with general reading. To find materials, it is usually recommended that the debaters begin with general indexes leading to books and articles that provide an overview of the topic. Some general indexes are:

> *Humanities Index* ***
> *New York Times Index* ***
> *PAIS (Public Affairs Information Service)* ***
> *Periodical Abstracts* ***
> *Readers' Guide to Periodical Literature* ***
> *Social Sciences Index* ***

Topic Oriented Research

Once the debaters have a better understanding about their topic, they can begin searching for more specialized books and articles that affirm or rebut the argument or proposition. Depending on the direction of their focus, they will choose from titles like:

> *America History and Life* ***
> *Education Index* ***
> *Historical Abstracts* ***
> *Sociological Abstracts* ***
> *Statistical Universe* ***

Argument Specific Research

Each debater must be prepared to make an affirmative, supporting constructive speech that is followed by another student who makes the first negative rebuttal. What generally follows is an affirmative rebuttal, another negative rebuttal, and then the final affirmative rebuttal. It is easy to understand that a great deal of library research and reading is necessary in order to locate and digest the materials. This is not an assignment that can be done the night before the debate.

The Greenhaven Press has been publishing a series of debate anthologies on contemporary issues for 25 years in the Opposing Viewpoints Series. The format of this series includes a brief introduction to the topic, articles by experts in the field, and a bibliography. Students will be exposed to various sides of a debate, which promotes issue awareness and critical thinking, classroom discussion, and the basis for individual research. See also the section below that discusses publisher's series.

Components of the Instruction and Training

Below are points that you should consider as you plan and prepare for an instruction session.

- Include an introduction to searching for information that will provide background and overviews as well as look at both the affirmative and negative aspects of issues.
- Instructors should be experienced and knowledgeable about general information resources and how to search electronic resources.
- Reserve the library's electronic teaching center for your presentations. If one is not available, reserve a library classroom.
- Ideally, the session should include an LCD panel, overhead projector, and a sufficient number of workstations to let trainees engage in hands-on activities.
- Make sure all software is loaded and working on the demo computer.
- Make bookmarks for Web sites you will use. Emphasize that all information is **NOT** on the Web; effective reference work requires skill in using BOTH print and electronic information sources.
- Spend some time in preparing your lesson plans, decide what the instructional goals will be and write the instructional objectives.
- Decide if you will use an evaluation of the training's effectiveness.
- Photocopy or create any materials that will be used—handouts, worksheets, and transparencies.
- Select examples of resources to discuss.
- Discuss the concepts of keyword and subject searching.

Searching the Catalog

Subject and keyword searching in the catalog will have to become rather creative because there are not any direct headings that lead into two sides. The best strategy might be to use a keyword search with the "topic" and words like "debate(s)" or "issue(s)" or "argument(s)." It is always productive to use both the official headings from the Library of Congress and from the Sears lists as well as any words that are commonly used to express the topic idea.

Searching Bibliographies

A first step in any research is to find out what resources are available on the subject being investigated. The use of a bibliography is an efficient way of discovering relevant materials. Many hundreds of bibliographic resources have been compiled on most every conceivable topic. These works are generally arranged by subject headings. The *Bibliographic Index* is a useful compilation of listings on many topics. Bibliographies on specific topics must be search by subject headings. Articles and chapters in books may include bibliographic references that will provide leads for further searching. See also the chapter in this book by Lawrence L. Tomikel that covers Bibliographies.

Publisher's Series

At Issue Series (Greenhaven Press)

Books in this anthology series focus a wide range of viewpoints into a single controversial issue (one example is the ethics of euthanasia), providing in-depth discussion by leading advocates. These books offer the reader a full spectrum of dissent on the subject. Extensive bibliographies and annotated lists of relevant organizations to contact offer avenues for further research.—*Greenhaven Press Catalog Winter 1999.*

Contemporary Issues Companion (Greenhaven Press)

This new series provides readers with information on topics of current interest. Each anthology examines an important social issue (one example is legalized gambling) in a variety of ways from personal accounts and case studies to pertinent factual and statistical articles to commentaries and overviews. Each includes relevant primary sources, introductory essays, summaries of every article, current book and periodical bibliographies, lists of organizations to contact, and extensive indexes.—*Greenhaven Press Catalog Winter 1999.*

Contemporary Issues Series (Prometheus Books)

Each title assembles a wide range of views in the ongoing public debates on issues like drugs or suicide. For example, in the title that discusses drugs, the ethical issues as well as anthropological, sociological, economic, political, and philosophical questions are addressed. Many of the chapters were written by authorities in the field especially for the series while others have been reprinted with permission.

Contemporary World Issues (ABC-CLIO)

The titles in this series cover social, political, environmental, and economic issues facing the world today. They all have the subtitle "a reference handbook." Each book contains an overview of the subject, a detailed chronology, biographical sketches, facts and data and/or documents and other primary source material, a directory of organizations and agencies, annotated lists of print and nonprint resources, a glossary, and an index. They are written by scholars and nonacademic experts to provide a starting point for research by high school and college students, the general public, and scholars.

Current Controversies (Greenhaven Press)

The books in this series examine timely national and international social, political, and economic debates that are often controversial. Each title presents diverse perspectives on the many sides of each issue presented through a variety of articles and book excerpts. Each chapter includes an overview, some are concise whereas the longer chapters are more expansive. Each book includes primary sources, annotated tables of contents, book and chapter introductions, indexes and bibliographies, and lists of organizations to contact.

CQ Researcher (Congressional Quarterly Inc.)

48 reports are issued each year. Each provides background on a current topic of widespread interest and is designed as a starting place for research. The reports define the issues and include a chronology and extensive bibliographies, as well as organizations where the reader can get additional information. A feature called "At Issue" which quotes opposing viewpoints from two experts is part of each report. *Editorial Research Reports* was the title until 1991.

Opposing Viewpoints Series (Greenhaven Press)

Each title explores a specific issue by placing expert opinions in a pro/con format. The viewpoints are selected from a wide range of respected publications including both popular and unpopular viewpoints. The selections made by the editorial team expose readers to many sides of a debate that promotes issue awareness as well as critical thinking. Each chapter will include about six articles that take **pro and con** points-of-view. Many include a periodical bibliography to supplement the diverse views presented in the chapter. At the end of a volume, there will be a listing of organizations concerned with the issues debated in the book and a bibliography of books cited in the chapters.—*Greenhaven Press Catalog, Winter 1999*. The publisher also has the *Opposing Viewpoints Juniors* series.

Greenhaven Press has published two supplementary texts for use with this series: *A Guide to Argumentative Writing* (1996) and *Writing Research Papers* (1998. 2d ed.). Each contains classroom activities, exercises, assignments, and an instructor's guide.

The Reference Shelf (H.W. Wilson Co.)

This series contains reprints of articles, excerpts from books, and addresses on current issues and social trends in the United States and other countries. There are six separately bound numbers to each volume, all of which are generally published in the same year. One number is a collection of recent speeches, each of the others is devoted to a single subject and gives background information and discussion from various points of view, concluding with a comprehensive bibliography.

Introductory Texts

Argument and Research, by James D. Lester (1999)
The Debater's Guide, by H.M. Ericson & J.J. Murphy (1987)
Elements of Argument, by Annette T. Rottenberg (2000)
Structure of Argument, by Annette T. Rottenberg (2000)
Pros and Cons, by Trevor Sather (1999)

Hands-on Exercises with a "Pro-Con" Approach

Background reading usually begins with the best available general works on a topic or issue and then proceeds to references on specific aspects. The exercises in this chapter begin with a step that is just beyond the first readings.

The 12 topics that are included deal with health and social issues in the United States today. The assumption is made that the participants have access to the titles in the Opposing Viewpoints Series published by Greenhaven Press. If they are not available, substitute some other sources for specialized background reading.

drug abuse	sports in America
abortion	suicide
America's children	health care
child abuse	elderly
family	population
homelessness	poverty

If a class has less than 12 participants, each can be assigned an individual topic. If there are more than 12, assign pairs or teams to carry out the search strategy exercise.

Two worksheets are included in the chapter. The remaining exercises are only on the accompanying disk; they may be customized in any way to meet the needs in individual libraries.

Debate Topic Exercise

A student has to participate in a debate in a public speaking class and doesn't have a clue how to begin.

As the librarian at the reference desk, set up a strategy for the student to research the pros and cons of a sub-topic of "drug abuse." Use print, electronic, and Web resources.

Step 1   Focus this library activity on one of the questions listed below. Select the one of most concern to you or which you think will present the best pro and con arguments to complete the requirement of this class.

> How serious a problem is drug abuse?
> How should the war on drugs be waged?
> Should drug testing be used in the workplace?
> How should prescription drugs be regulated?
> How can drug abuse be reduced?

Step 2   The next step is to read background information on the sub-topic.

Locate the book *Drug Abuse* (1994) published by Greenhaven Press. The chapter titles of this book are the questions listed above. Each chapter will include about six articles, which take pro and con points-of-view. This book will be a good starting place for background information on the topic. Another title to examine by the same publisher is *Legalizing Drugs* (1996).

Examine the bibliographies located at the end of this book. The additional readings may be useful for further information on this topic.

Search to see if your library has *CQ Researcher*. The reports issued in this title include a brief but thorough examination of this topic, a chronological overview, and bibliographies useful for further research. "Drug Testing; Does It Deter Drug Abuse?"—November 20, 1998; "Treating Addiction"—January 6, 1995; "Preventing Teen Drug Abuse. Do School Programs Push the Wrong Message?"—July 28, 1995; and "Teens and Tobacco; Do Cigarette Ads Encourage Teens to Start Smoking?" in December 1, 1995.

Search to see if your library has this title: *Drug Abuse in Society; a Reference Handbook* (1993). This book is published as part of a series called "Contemporary World Issues" and includes an overview of the problem, a chronology that goes from the pre-colonial era right to the 1990s, as well as some facts and statistics. *Illegal Drugs* (1998) is part of the "Contemporary Issues" series.

Step 3   Make a list of keywords that are essential for further searching on this topic.

Step 4   Analyze your focus to determine which disciplines publish articles in the scholarly journals. The indexes of most disciplines are available in both print and electronic versions.

If the medical point of view is taken, articles will have been written in the medical literature and you can search those on the *Medline* database.

If it is from a sociological point of view, search *Sociological Abstracts*.

A government or policy perspective would be covered in *PAIS* and if the U.S. government has studied the question, it will be accessed through databases that cover government publications like *MOCAT*.

If the focus is from an angle not yet mentioned, speculate about it and then discuss the best database with a reference librarian.

Step 5   Search the online catalog for any titles you identified in the additional readings mentioned in Step 2.

Search the online catalog for additional titles using the keywords you compiled and used to search for scholarly articles in periodical indexes,.

Step 6   Need more up-to-date information? *CQ Researcher* regularly lists, in its reports, agencies, interest groups, and organizations to contact.

Step 7   Search the Internet for information about the topic. Perhaps the agencies listed in some of the previous references will be good places to begin this step. List several sites that appear to have information that will further your research.

Debate Topic Exercise

A student has to participate in a debate in a public speaking class and doesn't have a clue how to begin.

*As the librarian at the reference desk, set up a strategy for the student to research the pros and cons of a sub-topic of **"the elderly in America**." Use print, electronic, and Web resources.*

Step 1   The questions listed below are all sub-topics relating to the elderly. Focus this library activity on one that relates to the elderly in America:

> How does society view the elderly?
> Are the elderly poor?
> Is Social Security necessary for the elderly?
> How should society meet the elderly's health care needs?

Step 2   Read background information on the sub-topic.

Locate the books *The Elderly* (1990) and *An Aging Population* (1996) published by Greenhaven Press. The chapter titles of these books are the questions from which you selected your focus. Each chapter will include about six articles, which take pro and con points-of-view. Another title to consult is *Generations Apart: Xers vs Boomers vs the Elderly* (1997). These books will be a starting place for information on the focus of your topic.

Also look at the bibliographies located in these books. The additional readings may be useful to you for further information.

Search to see if your library has *CQ Researcher*. In the July 24, 1992 issue, there is a report called "At Issue: Is a Federally Funded Program the Best Way to Provide Long-Term Care for the Elderly?" The February 20, 1998 issue covers "Caring for the Elderly. Is Adequate Long-term Care Available?" and the May 15, 1998 issue includes "Alzheimer's Disease. Can It Bankrupt the Health-care System?" These reports include a brief but thorough examination of the topic, a chronological overview, and bibliographies you will find useful for further research.

The 1994 *Britannica Yearbook* (p.144) featured an article on financial support for the elderly.

Step 3   Construct a list of relevant terms, keywords, or concepts that describe facets of this topic; they are essential for further searching on this research project.

Step 4   Analyze your focus to determine which disciplines publish articles in the scholarly journals. The indexes of most disciplines are available in both print and electronic versions.

If the point of view of sociology is taken, articles will have been written in sociology related literature and you can search those in *Sociological Abstracts*.

If it is from a medical point of view, search the *Medline* database.

A government or policy perspective would be covered in *PAIS* and if the U.S. government has studied the question, it will be accessed through indexes that cover government publications like *MOCAT*.

If the focus is from an angle not yet mentioned, speculate about it and then discuss the best database with a reference librarian.

Step 5   Search the online catalog for any titles you identified in the additional readings mentioned in Step 2.

Search the online catalog for additional titles using the keywords you compiled and used to search for scholarly articles in periodical indexes,.

Step 6   Need more up-to-date information? *CQ Researcher* regularly lists, in its reports, agencies, interest groups, and organizations to contact.

Step 7   Search the Internet for information about the topic. Perhaps the agencies listed in some of the previous references will be good places to begin this step. List several sites that appear to have information that will further your research.

Environmental Sciences

JOHN P. MCDONOUGH
Supervisor, Current Periodicals
UNIVERSITY OF PITTSBURGH HILLMAN LIBRARY

MARILYN P. WHITMORE
Editor
LIBRARY INSTRUCTION PUBLICATIONS

Introduction

It is only in the most recent, and brief, period of their tenure that human beings have developed in sufficient numbers, and acquired enough power, to become one of the most potentially dangerous organisms that the planet has ever hosted.—*John McHale*

The environmental crisis is an outward manifestation of a crisis of mind and spirit. There could be no greater misconception of its meaning than to believe it is concerned only with endangered wildlife, human-made ugliness, and pollution. These are part of it, but more importantly, the crisis is concerned with the kind of creatures we are and what we must become in order to survive.—*Lynton K. Caldwell*

The problems that overwhelm us today are precisely those we failed to solve decades ago.—*M.K. Tolba*

Environmental science is extremely interdisciplinary, drawing upon many of the physical sciences such as biology, chemistry, geology, paleoclimatology, mathematics, statistics, meteorology, and oceanography. For example, "to comprehend the intricacies of the dangers of radioactive and toxic waste disposal to animal life and to water supplies, one must be familiar with hydrology, nuclear physics, chemistry, soil science, ecology, biology, risk analysis, and demography."—*Reading about the Environment, by Pamela E. Jansma.* Environmental studies also rely heavily on social sciences such as economics, politics, and ethics.

Answering questions related to the complexities surrounding today's environmental issues may pose difficulties. The subject area is vast and it is virtually impossible to prepare for the myriad of questions that may be asked by a library patron at the reference desk. While many of the questions relating to the environmental arena are asked by the nonspecialist and are fairly basic, a reasonably strong science background would be of benefit in more complex areas. This list highlights just a few of the most prevalent current environmental issues.
- Waste management and pollution control,
- Natural resources and the impacts of their ever increasing consumption,
- Endangered species and biodiversity,
- Greenhouse effect and global warming,

- Global deforestation,
- Synthetic chemicals and their environmental impacts,
- Recycling and its benefits, and
- Global overpopulation.

Circumstances for the Instruction

For several decades there has been an explosion of information about every aspect of the environment. Every week the media details some kind of environmental catastrophe. The public seeks more information but may feel bewildered by the overwhelming array of books and magazine articles in libraries. Knowing the proper terminology when starting an information search is probably the single most important part. Library staff at all levels must have a basic knowledge of resources in order to provide assistance. Training is the key to their success.

When a training or instruction session is being planned, it is recommended that the following be considered for inclusion in the presentation.
- Key environmental sciences reference resources, i.e., dictionaries, encyclopedias, bibliographies, handbooks, statistics, etc. Some of these will be available in electronic format and it is essential that the instructor be aware of them.
- Key reference resources that cover specific environmental topics, i.e., air quality, greenhouse effect, industrial waste, population/overpopulation, recycling, water, weather, wildlife, etc.
- International resources that cover any of the above aspects. Especially UN information sources because the United Nations has been increasingly involved with environmental concerns since 1972.
- Electronic gateways that allow users to link to the home pages of national, state, and local governments, international organizations or agencies, and regional organizations or agencies.
- Sites that present tips about how to evaluate electronic gateways. Examine the one by Esther Grassian—http://www.library.ucla.edu/libraries/college/instruct/critical.htm.

Components of the Instruction

Below are points that you should consider as you plan and prepare for an instruction session.
- Instructors should be experienced and knowledgeable about information resources that cover the environmental sciences.
- Reserve the library's electronic teaching center for your presentations. If one is not available, reserve a library classroom.
- Ideally, the session should include an LCD panel, overhead projector, and a sufficient number of workstations to let participants engage in hands-on activities.
- Make sure all software is loaded and working on the demo computer.

- Make bookmarks for Web sites you will use. Emphasize that all environmental information is **NOT** on the Web; effective reference work requires skill in using BOTH print and electronic information sources.
- Spend some time in preparing your lesson plans, decide what the instructional goals will be and write the instructional objectives.
- Decide how to follow through and make an evaluation of the training's effectiveness.
- Photocopy or create any materials that will be used—handouts, worksheets, and transparencies. You may wish to design a web-page for the training.
- Select examples of environmental sources to discuss. You may decide to use earlier editions of titles so reference work won't be hampered because the latest editions have been taken from the ready-reference collection.
- Discuss the concepts of subject and keyword searching.
- Discuss and show trainees, perhaps on the overhead, how to search for key Library of Congress Subject Headings (or Sears if that is more appropriate). There are many dozens of subject headings for environmental topics. Selected examples are listed:

    Analysis of environmental impact USE ⇒ Environmental impact analysis
    Chemical pollutants USE ⇒ Pollutants
    Environmental action groups USE ⇒ Green movement
    Environmental assessment USE ⇒ Analysis of environmental impact
    Environmental economics—[geographic subdivision]
    Environmental engineering—[geographic subdivision]
    Environmental groups USE ⇒ Green movement
    Environmental health—[geographic subdivision]
    Environmental impact analysis—[geographic subdivision]
    Environmental law—[geographic subdivision]
    Environmental policy—[geographic subdivision]
    Environmental protection—[geographic subdivision]
    Environmental responsibility—[geographic subdivision]
    Environmental change USE ⇒ Global environmental change
    Global warming
    Green movement—[geographic subdivision]
    Man—Influence on nature
    Pollution—[geographic subdivision]
    Pollutants—[geographic subdivision]
    Protection of environment USE ⇒ Environmental protection

- At the beginning of each session, initiate introductions. Tell the participants what the general objectives will be, e.g., acquiring basic knowledge about environmental sciences information sources, and how to access them.

Selected Reference Resources for Environmental Sciences

Each environmental issue—air, water, waste, recycling, energy, etc.—has its own literature including dictionaries, directories, handbooks, manuals, abstracts, etc. Most of the examples included in this chapter are more general. When your research needs dictate a single issue, search for resources under the particular issue.

Those sources that are also in electronic format (CD-ROM, Internet subscription) will be marked with a triple asterisk ***. The resources are arranged in the following categories:
    Almanacs and Yearbooks
    Atlases
    Bibliographies and Guides to the Literature
    Biographies
    Chronologies
    Dictionaries
    Directories
    Encyclopedias
    Handbooks and Manuals
    Introductory Readings and Overviews
    Indexes and Abstracts
    Additional Relevant Internet Sites
    Environmental Policy and Plans
    Quotations
    Research and Information Organizations/Agencies
    Statistics
    Manuals for Action

Almanacs and Yearbooks

European Environmental Almanac. 1995.
The first part of the volume presents an overview of Europe's environment. The remainder contains country profiles, arranged alphabetically by country.

State of the World, 1984– (annual)
The Worldwatch Institute annual report emphasizes the important environmental crises and issues of that year. It provides a collection of facts, figures, and anecdotes about what is happening to our planet in regard to solid waste recycling, renewable energy, deforestation, extinction of species, toxic chemicals, and population. The Institute is an organization that monitors the impact of economic development on the environment and the world's progress towards sustainable development. This report is an excellent source of up-to-date information on environmental problems.

Atlases

Atlas of Environmental Issues. 1989.
Facts on File produced this easy-to-understand atlas for young readers from the sixth grade upward.

Atlas of the Environment. 1996 ed.
This global environmental atlas presents the basic facts about the natural and human environments, and what is happening to them. The text, written to be understood by

those with no previous background in the subject, is accompanied by maps and charts, and graphs.—*Introd.*

The New State of the Earth Atlas; A Concise Survey of the Environment through Full-Color International Maps. 1995.
The world is portrayed in maps by environmental variables. The same information is then shown in tabular form, and the last part of the volume is a verbal description again arranged by the variables.

World Wildlife Federation Atlas of the Environment. 1994.
Earlier atlases have portrayed nature as it affects humanity, the maps in this volume show how people are affecting nature. Topics that are described include the world's forests, wetlands, deserts, croplands, mountains, rivers, etc. The threats to them are detailed. A bibliography of sources is listed at the end.

Some additional selected atlases to consult are:
The Environment of the British Isles (1995)
The Great Lakes: An Environmental Atlas and Resource Book (1995)
World Atlas of Desertification (1997)
World Bank Atlas (1967–)

Bibliographies and Guides to the Literature
Argus Clearinghouse; A Selective Collection of Topical Guides
http://www.lib.umich.edu/chhome.html
Select **Environment** for a guide to environmental resources on the Internet.

Beacham's Guide to Environmental Issues and Sources. 1993.
This 5-volume work is a comprehensive bibliography of books and periodical articles on many environmental topics covering 1988 through 1993. The arrangement is according to environmental topic and, within each of these categories by type of resource.

The Catalog of Hazardous & Solid Waste Publications. 1999.
This catalog provides an alphabetical listing of the most frequently requested publications originating from the Office of Solid Waste. It also lists sources from which they are available.

The Environmentalist's Bookshelf; A Guide to the Best Books. 1993.
The listings include classic titles like *Silent Spring* (by Rachel Carson who alerted us to the harmful effects of overuse of pesticides and helped launch the environmental movement) and *The Limits to Growth* (written by a group of MIT scientists who warned about the ecological disasters that could result from uncontrolled human population growth and natural resources consumption). Robert Merideth surveyed 236 environmental leaders to come up with this list of the 500 most acclaimed environmental books.

Guide to Environment and Development Sources of Information on CD-ROM and the Internet. 1998.
This is a publication of the United Nations Development Programme. It is divided into two broad subject and country sections. There are three indexes to the entries: a listing by broad subject headings; a subject index using narrower subject terms, and a title index.

Reading about the Environment; An Introductory Guide. 1993.
This title offers annotations of books and articles for the nonspecialist. Some of the chapter titles are: the human relationship to the environment, overpopulation, air pollution, acid rain, ozone depletion, water pollution, toxic waste, pesticides, cosmetics, food additives, radiation, land mismanagement, and noise pollution. Each chapter begins with a summary essay that outlines the important aspects of the topic covered. Also described are works that are good general overviews for the individual who wishes to become knowledgeable about the topic. Citations the author believes to be especially noteworthy have symbols to indicate a good overview, scholarly treatment, or an excellent factual source.—*Introd.*

The Sierra Club Green Guide; Everybody's Desk Reference to Environmental Information. 1996.
This guide is divided into two parts: Environmental Issues and Green Living. It features more than 1,200 essential resources including Internet sites, bulletin board systems, and electronic databases to help the reader answer any environmental question.

Some additional titles to consult are:
Bibliographic Index
Bibliographic Guide to the Environment, 1993–
Current Contents. Agriculture, Biology, and Environmental Sciences ***
Environmental Periodicals Bibliography ***
EPA Publications (U.S. Environmental Protection Agency)

Biographies

Environmental Heroes—Success Stories of People at Work for the Earth. 1996.
Profiles of people involved in recycling and composting projects as well as other environmental issues are included.

The Environmentalists: A Biographical Dictionary from the 17ᵗʰ Century to the Present. 1993.
This is an annotated listing of some 500 individuals from the U.S. and abroad who are significant to the environment movement in some way. Many photographs are included. It also includes about 100 major environmental organizations and agencies.

Pioneer Conservationists of Eastern America. 1986.

Pioneer Conservationists of Western America. 1979.
Fifteen biographies are included in each of the two titles. Some famous names included are John Muir, Theodore Roosevelt, Rachel Carson, Franklin Delano Roosevelt, and Ralph Nader.

Women Pioneers for the Environment. 1998.
"From the beginning of the more recent environmental movement, women have been the force driving grassroots activism."—*Pref.* The author states that this book of about 40 stories is merely a sampling of 19th and 20th century women environmental activists from around the world. She has tried to achieve a geographical and ethnic balance.

Who's Who in Environmental Engineering, 1955– (annual)
The information provided is brief as in other who's who type works. All biographees must be certified by the American Academy of Environmental Engineers.

World Who Is Who and Does What in Environment & Conservation. 1997.
The alphabetical listings form the main body of the work and include the biographee's qualifications and affiliations, educational background and pertinent work experience, achievements and awards, and specialist interests and publications. An Appendix lists biographees by country and by specialty.

Try more general sources if the resources listed above are not available at your library.
 American Men & Women of Science
 Biography Index
 Canadian Who's Who
 Current Biography
 International Who's Who
 Who's Who in America

Chronologies
Chronology of 20th Century History: Ecology and the Environment. 1997.
The 2-volume title is encyclopedic in nature. It addresses major twentieth century environmental issues by examining key historical incidents and developments in the environmental sciences and related fields.—*Pref.*

Some additional titles to consult are:
A Chronology of Weather (1998)
Earth Shock (1993)
National Geographic Eyewitness to the 20th Century (1998)
Protecting Tokyo's Environment (1985)
Wilderness Preservation (1994)

Dictionaries

A Dictionary of Ecology. 1999 ed.
Michael Allaby provides clear definitions of thousands of terms from the fields of ecology, biology, chemistry, geology, oceanography, toxicology, and climatology. It contains extensive cross references.

Dictionary of the Environment. 1990 ed.
This general dictionary by Michael Allaby explains terminology from a broad spectrum of environmental sciences. It will be an indispensable aid for the person overwhelmed by terminology from many disciplines.

Dictionary of Environment and Sustainable Development. 1996.
Alan Gilpin includes about 2,000 entries that define terms and concepts relating to the whole span of environmental issues. The emphasis is on international conventions, environmental law, environmental evolution in many countries, pollution control, environmental impact assessment, sustainable development, and intergenerational equity.—*Back cover.*

Dictionary of Environmental Science and Technology. 1996 ed.
This dictionary provides both the student and the general reader with a working knowledge of the scientific and technical terminology associated with environmental studies and appraisals of current issues. Many of the entries are covered in some depth; diagrams and tables are used to embellish the text.

Earth Words. 1995.
A work for the young reader, this title defines words and terms commonly used in discussing the environment from "acid rain" to "wetland."

Environment Dictionary. 1998.
David Kemp provides short definitions that are accompanied by illustrations, diagrams, maps, tables, etc., as appropriate. Many include listings of further readings. International agencies are included with brief descriptions of their foci.

Glossary of Environment Statistics. 1996.
A United Nations document—UN Docs: UN/ST/ESA/STAT/Ser F/67

Illustrated Dictionary of Environmental Health & Occupational Safety. 1996.
Over 7,500 terms drawn from varied specialized and technical fields are related in such a matter as to be accessible to both professionals and general readers. Drawings, diagrams, and charts are used to further explain terms.—*Pref.*

Directories

Canadian Environmental Directory, 1991–
This title is considered an outstanding and comprehensive guide to Canadian sources of environmental information. It covers government agencies, Canadian and international

organizations, research laboratories, special libraries, journalists, products and services. There is also a bibliography of directories, databases, books, and newsletters.

Encyclopedia of Environmental Sources. 1993.
This search tool is arranged by a "comprehensive and detailed list" of very specific and narrowly defined environmental topics. Within each topic, the entries are arranged alphabetically by type of source and by publication title or organization name.

Environmental Industries Marketplace. 1992.
EIM is a comprehensive guide to manufacturers and providers of environmental regulatory products and services in the United States. Contact and descriptive information is provided on nearly 11,000 companies. It is arranged in three sections—alphabetical, subject, and geographic.

Environmental Profiles: A Global Guide to Projects and People. 1993.
More than 1,500 environmental organizations in 115 countries are summarized; about one-third are U.S organizations. A detailed index identifies people, issues, species, legislation, and organizations.

Environmental Telephone Directory, 1986– (annual)
This is an essential resource for anyone who needs to contact state or federal officials about environmental laws, regulations, policies, and court decisions.

GreenWorld's Almanac and Directory of Environmental Organizations, 1994–
Volume 1 provides descriptions of about 700 organizations in the U.S. and Canada. The title is categorized according to field of focus. The listings include mission statements, memberships, geographical coverage, affiliations, fees, funding, major sponsors, programs and activities, and publication titles.

Directory for the Environment: Organizations, Campaigns and Initiatives in the British Isles. 1990 ed.
This compilation describes about 1,500 environmental and conservation organizations in the UK; addresses and telephone numbers are included.

Directory of European Environmental Organizations. 1993 ed.
There are two sections, governmental organizations and non-governmental organizations. Under each entry, one will find the founding date, purpose, organization, activities, publications, etc.

Environment Encyclopedia and Directory. 1998 ed.
This is a multipurpose sourcebook of international environmental information. World and regional maps highlight environmental issues, definitions of terms and events, descriptions of environmental organizations from around the world, an extensive annotated bibliography of periodicals, and biographical details for key individuals in the environmental movement. The bulk of the book is the directory of organizations.

Gale Environmental Sourcebook, 1992– (biennial)
This resource is designed as a guide "to organizations, agencies, programs, publications, and other resources that study, define, and report on the environment."—*Introd.*

National Wildlife Federation Conservation Directory. 1999.
The title includes over 3,000 agencies, organizations, and universities with conservation programs. It also contains more than 18,000 officials involved with environmental conservation, natural resource management, and education.

World Directory of Environmental Organizations, 1973– (irregularly updated)
This is the most comprehensive worldwide listing of organizations; more than 200 countries are represented. National, international, governmental and non-governmental organizations are included. The directory also includes a glossary and a chronology of landmark events.

If your library does not own any of the above specialized directories, consult the *Encyclopedia of Associations* or the online version called *Associations Unlimited.*

Encyclopedias

Conservation and Environmentalism; An Encyclopedia. 1995.
Entries for about 500 terms from a broad range of fields are included. They range from short to several pages and each includes the name of the author, a list of further readings, and suggestions of other headings to consult.

Encyclopedia of Ecology and Environmental Management. 1998.
This work seeks to be both a dictionary and an encyclopedia; the editors consider it a good starting point for those who know little and want a broad coverage of the jargon and the principles. The short and long definitions are signed and most include a listing of references. Maps graphs, charts, and other illustrations have been included to enhance the text.

Environment Encyclopedia, 1994– (biennial)
Every aspect of the interdisciplinary field of environmental sciences seems to be covered. It was produced for a lay audience and includes clear definitions and discussion. There are numerous charts and graphs and a detailed index.

Macmillan Encyclopedia of the Environment. 1997.
This lavishly illustrated, 6-volume set will appeal to students and laypersons interested in environmental topics, legislation, ecology, and evolution. Major environmental legislation, organizations, and U.S. governmental agencies with environmental responsibilities are listed in appendixes.

Try more general sources if the resources listed above are not available at your library.
Encyclopedia Americana ***
McGraw-Hill Encyclopedia of Science and Technology
The New Encyclopaedia Britannica ***
Van Nostrand's Scientific Encyclopedia ***
World Book Encyclopedia ***

There are two illustrated encyclopedias for the very young if your library serves that age.
The Grolier Student Encyclopedia of Science, Technology, and the Environment
The Raintree Illustrated Science Encyclopedia

Handbooks and Manuals

ABC-CLIO Companion to the Environmental Movement. 1994.
This is a guide for the nonspecialist to the conservation movement and environmentalism from the nation's early naturalists to the present. It includes information on conservationists, environmental activists, key government officials, government and private institutions and organizations, landmark legislation and court decision, concepts, and watershed events.—*Pref.*

The Complete Book of Home Environmental Hazards. 1990.
This manual is divided into three parts: environmental hazards inside the home, environmental hazards outside the home, and what to look for when keeping a house to make sure it is environmentally sound. The first two parts are arranged by the topic such as asbestos, lead, hazardous waste sites, etc. A short glossary has been included as well as helpful telephone numbers for both the United States and Canada.

Cooper's Comprehensive Environmental Desk Reference with a Supplemental Spell Check Disk. 1996 ed.
Cooper's is a specialized reference to the standard jargon used by environmentalists, planners, compliance officers, bureaucrats, professionals and others in the field. It is arranged in eight sections:
* I is the alphabetical list of environmental terms
* II lists hundreds of environmental acronyms and abbreviations
* III is a Sample Phase I Environmental Site Assessment that can be used for student instruction or professional reference
* IV is a reference to the Hazardous Air Pollutants (HAPs) List that is found in the Clean Air Act
* V provides environmental data conversion tables
* VI lists chemical elements and abbreviations
* VII provides information on EPA offices and programs
* VIII is a topical index of selected terms included in the book

Environment in Key Words; A Multilingual Handbook of the Environment. 1990.
This 2-volume set is in English, French, German, and Russian. It is arranged in three sections with vocabulary from the natural and social sciences as well as economics and politics to cover the interdisciplinary nature of environmental concerns. Volume 1

includes (a) The ecological balance; (b) Description of the ecological balance; and (3) Some measures for the re-establishment of the ecological balance. Volume 2 is an index to the terms in the sections of Volume 1.

Environmentally Induced Disorders Sourcebook. 1997.
This title provides basic information for the lay person about diseases and syndromes linked to exposure to pollutants and other substances in both outdoor and indoor environments. These include lead, asbestos, formaldehyde, mercury, emissions, noise, and more.

Hazardous Substances Resource Guide. 1996 ed.
This book contains introductory chapters on chemical hazards and extensive lists of resources to additional information plus profiles outlining the potential dangers and storage of more than 1,000 hazardous substances found in and around the home, workplace, and community. The profiles contain a minimum of technical and medical jargon.—*Pref.*

Recycling Sourcebook: A guide to Recyclable Materials, Case Studies, Organizations, Agencies, and Publications. 1993.
The *Sourcebook* includes an overview of recycling in the 1990's, information on 13 types of recyclable materials, case studies and how-to information on programs. Contact and descriptive information on some 4,000 resources that relate to recycling such as public interest groups, funding sources, government agencies, equipment suppliers, and publications are included.

Introductory Readings and Overviews

The Environment; A Revolution in Attitudes. 1998 ed. (biennial revisions)
The editors of the title provide a "State of the Environment" from the industrial revolution to NASA's mission to planet earth as an introduction. They also provide statistics, court decisions, state and federal laws, public opinion polls, and pro and con arguments where it is warranted for a multiplicity of specific topics. Some of those covered are global warming, ozone depletion, waste disposal, air quality, water issues, renewable energy, etc. The names and addresses of key agencies in the environmental field are provided. This is one of the titles in the Information Plus Reference Series written in easy to understand language for the general public as well as high school and college students.

Environmental Justice. 1995.
This title presents nine articles that argue various positions in the environmental justice issue. It is valuable because it presents opposing views on the topic; it also contains a bibliography and a list of organizations concerned with environmental justice.

Environmental Justice; A Reference Handbook. 1996
Within the last two decades, Americans have begun to realize there are special environmental problems facing minority and low-income communities. Out of this

realization has grown a new movement—the environmental justice movement. This book provides an overview of the subject, a detailed chronology, biographical sketches, facts and data and/or documents and other primary source material, a directory of organizations and agencies, annotated lists of print and nonprint resources, a glossary, and an index.

How Much Is Enough?: The Consumer Society and the Future of the Earth. 1992.
The author takes a thought-provoking look at consumerism. The emphasis is on the consumer class, especially the environmental costs of transportation, food production, consumption of raw materials, and waste generation.

Living in the Environment: An Introduction to Environmental Science. 1999 ed.
This is a widely used text on environmental studies with good references and examples plus a great deal of data. It covers topics such as ecology, demography, food supply, pollution, the use of environmental resources, and environmental economics and politics. It also includes opinion essays by leading environmentalists.

Living on the Earth. 1988.
This beautifully illustrated National Geographic Society publication describes the various habitats in which humans live. These include: the arctic; islands; forests; grasslands; rivers; highlands, and coasts. Some of the photographs included spotlight the intrusion of modern society into pristine wild land.

Opposing Viewpoints Series.
A series of books published by Greenhaven Press where opposing viewpoints are placed back to back to allow the reader to follow a continuing debate throughout each book. The materials in the chapters are selected from magazines, newspapers, and books; some have been written expressly for the volume. Selected titles in this series that deal with environmental topics are listed below:
>*Endangered Species* (1996)
>*Energy Alternatives* (1991)
>*The Environment* (1996)
>*Garbage and Waste* (1997)
>*Global Resources* (1998)
>*Global Warming* (1997)
>*Issues in the Environment* (1998)
>*Pollution* (1994)
>*Rainforests* (1998)
>*Water* (1994)

A Primer for Environmental Literacy. 1998.
The purpose of this book is to present key concepts of environmental science in a concise format that can be understood by those who are not natural scientists.—*Pref.*

Silent Spring. 1993 ed.
The classic title by Rachel Carson who is considered the grandmother of modern environmentalism. She is credited with making the public aware of the adverse health and environmental effects of chemicals, especially pesticides.

Water: The International Crisis. 1993.
This provides an overview of global freshwater scarcity issues.

Indexes and Abstracts
Ecological Abstracts ***
Ecology Abstracts ***
Both of these titles cover the international academic literature on the interaction of organisms with their environments.

EIS: Digests of Environmental Impact Statements, 1972– ***
EIS provides abstracts of all draft and final Environmental Impact Statements filed with the Environmental Protection Agency—approximately 500 each year. To keep current with the latest statements, readers must consult the *Federal Register.*

Environment Abstracts, 1971– ***
The title for the electronic version is *Enviroline.* The title summarizes articles on environmental sciences, conditions, and issues from more than 800 English-language scientific journals.

Environmental Periodicals Bibliography, 1973– ***
EPB lists the titles of articles found in popular, technical, and scientific environmental magazines and journals.

Try more subject oriented indexes/abstracts if the titles listed above do not provide the information you are searching.

Agriculture
AGRICOLA ***
Bibliography of Agriculture ***

Air
Global Climate Change Digest
Energy Research Abstracts ***

Biodiversity
Biological Abstracts ***
Wildlife Worldwide ***

Education
ERIC ***

Energy

Alternative Energy Digests ***
Energy Research Abstracts ***

Health and Toxics

NIOSHTIC (National Institute for Occupational Safety and Health)
Toxline ***

Pollution

Pollution Abstracts ***

Population

POPLINE ***

Waste

Hazardous Waste Superfund Database ***
Waste Information Digests

Water

Aquatic Sciences and Fisheries Abstracts ***
Biological Abstracts ***
Ground Water On-Line ***
Water Resources Abstracts ***
WATERNET ***
The Watershed Information Resource System ***

Try more general sources if the resources listed above are not available at your library.

Academic Universe ***
Expanded Academic ASAP ***
General Science Index ***
Monthly Catalog of United States Government Publications ***
National Newspaper Index ***
Periodical Abstracts ***
Readers' Guide to Periodical Literature ***
Science Citation Index ***

Additional Relevant Internet sites

American Public Information Center on the Environment
http://www.americanpie.org
APIE is an environmental organization that serves people and communities through a number of programs, including a toll-free telephone information line that responds to callers' environmental questions and concerns.

Committee for the National Institute for the Environment
http://www.cnie.org
This site provides population and environment linkages including environmental education programs and resources.

The Ecological Society of America Science & Environmental Policy Updates
http://esa.sdsc.edu/epupage.htm
The environmental policy updates are weekly summaries of the major environmental policy news.

Environment Canada
http://www.doe.ca/envhome.html
This is a useful resource for information about recycling in Canada.

Environmental Journals on the Internet
http://www.cnie.org/Journals.htm
Over 300 journals are grouped according to the amount of information provided online for free: full-text (43); table of contents + some articles (17); tables of contents + abstracts only (140); Table of contents only (102); and journal home page only (24).

Environmental Yellow Pages
http://www.cnie.org/yellow/

European Environmental Agency
Information on the environment can be accessed through the Europe server using
http://europa.eu.int/en/comm/dglldgllhome.html and http://www.eea.eu.int/

INFOTERRA
http://www.unep.org/unep/eia/en/infoterr/
This is the global environmental information exchange network of the United Nation's Environment Programme.

U.S. Environmental Protection Agency
http://www.epa.gov
This is the key agency of the U.S. government regarding environmental issues.

Virtual Library: Environment
http://earthsystems.org/Environment.shtml
This site has extensive links to sources on the environment.

Worldwatch Institute
http://www.worldwatch.org

For additional Web sites, search the institutions listed below. The *Gourman Report* lists them as having the best undergraduate and graduate programs in the environmental sciences. The Gourman listing and ranking is according to a subjective, quantifiable numeric system. Therefore, the listing below is alphabetical rather than the rank order in either of the Gourman titles.

Arizona University	University of Colorado at Boulder
California Institute of Technology	University of Florida
Clemson University	University of Illinois at Urbana/Champaign
Colorado State University	University of Massachusetts at Amherst

Cornell University
Georgia Institute of Technology
Harvard University
Indiana University at Bloomington
Purdue University
University of California at Berkeley
University of Cincinnati

University of Michigan at Ann Arbor
University of North Carolina at Chapel Hill
University of Pennsylvania
University of Texas at Austin
University of Wisconsin at Madison
Virginia Polytechnic Institute

Environmental Policy and Plans

The titles listed below represent a sample of those that have been published. Search the library catalog using the LC subject heading "Environmental policy—[name of country]" for additional titles.

Caring for Our Future: Action for Europe's Environment. 1998.
This publication is designed to raise public awareness and persuade citizens to help protect and management the environment; 25 themes are covered. First the reader is presented with the principal facts and trends followed by a brief discussion of the actions taken by European institutions and by a review of proposals currently under discussion. The final part of each theme examines individual players and their responsibility in the relevant field.—*Pref.* Colored photographs and graphs amplify the text.

The Environmental Protection System in Transition: Toward a More Desirable Future. 1998.
This is the final report of the Enterprise for the Environment's project that concentrates on United States environmental policy. Another title to consult is *American Foreign Environmental Policy and the Power of the State* (1998).

Environmental Restoration and Waste Management Plan: Five-Year Plan, 1991/95–
This plan is the cornerstone of the Department of Energy's long-term strategy in environmental restoration and waste management. Its purpose is to establish a department-wide agenda for cleanup and compliance against which overall progress can be measured. The first plan was issued in paper (SuDocs: E 1.60:) and the later ones are on microfiche (SuDocs: E 1.90/3:).—*Foreword*

The Next One Hundred Years; Shaping the Fate of Our Living Earth. 1990.
This is a summary of the state of the Earth at the close of the twentieth century and an estimate of the future of the planet. Most major environmental topics are discussed through interviews with scientists investigating the various phenomena. The author concludes that the situation for the survival of human beings is dire but that solutions are possible.

The State of Canada's Environment. 1991 ed.
The World Commission on Environment and Development urged nations to issue reports to serve as a tool for informed decision-making. Canada's report addresses four main questions. What is happening in Canada's environment? Why is it happening? Why is it significant? What are Canadians doing about it? The report is supplemented with maps, tables, graphs, and numerous other illustrations.

Vital Signs; The Trends That Are Shaping Our Future, 1992–
Beginning with the 1993 volume, the data published in the tables and used to chart the graphs have been also available on diskette. Each volume includes an overview, a discussion of key indicators, and special features of that year. The same topics are not necessarily featured in each publication.

The World Environment 1972–1992: Two Decades of Challenge. 1992.
Chief editor M.K. Tolba looks back over the past 20 years and reviews some of the trends and also looks into the future. The book looks at the environment from three perspectives. Ten introductory chapters detail the range of environmental threats and examine how they have unfolded. The second section reviews the different sectors of the economy, analyzing how each has impacted on the human environment. The final and major section analyses the range of responses to the changing environment. A range of national responses is examined and new international treaties are presented and their effectiveness evaluated.

Other selected titles to consult are:
> *Better Environmental Decisions; Strategies for Governments, Businesses, and Communities* (1999)
> *Environmental Policy in Transition: Making the Right Choices* (1996)
> *The Global Casino: An Introduction to Environmental Issues* (1995)
> *Impact of Environmental Assessment: A Review of World Bank Experience* (1997)

Quotations

A Dictionary of Environmental Quotations. 1992.
Approximately 4,000 quotations have been taken from books, articles, speeches, and bumper stickers. Each quotation includes the name of the author, occasion or publication title, and date. There are author and subject indexes. This book is fun to browse and useful for writing speeches, term papers, and articles.

Research and Information Organizations/Agencies
There are many hundreds of organizations and agencies concerned with environmental issues in the world. Those listed below are a small sample.

- Environmental Protection Agency (EPA) was established in 1970 to coordinate U.S. governmental action on environmental issues—http://www.epa.gov. It has an extensive list of publications that can be identified through the *Monthly Catalog of United States Government Publications ***.*
- Fish and Wildlife Service
- International Union for Conservation of Nature and Natural Resources
- National Academy of Sciences

- United National Environment Programme was formed at the UN Conference on the Human Environment in 1972. It coordinates international measures for monitoring and protecting the environment.
- Sierra Club
- U.S. Department of Agriculture
- U.S. Department of the Interior
- U.S. Geological Survey
- World Bank
- World Wildlife Fund
- Worldwatch Institute is an independent, nonprofit research organization created to analyze and to focus on global problems.

Statistics

Environmental Data Report, 1989/90– (biennial)
This is considered the most comprehensive collection of country-by-country statistical data. All United National Environment Programme member countries are included.

Eurostat Yearbook. 1986–1996 ed.
The yearbook is for and about Europeans. It compares significant features of each country of the European Union and, in turn, of the European countries, those in EFTA and the United States of America, Canada, and Japan.—*Pref.*

Health and Environment in America's Top-Rated Cities; A Statistical Profile, 1994/95–
The cities were chosen based on their rankings in various surveys as being the best places for business and living in the United States. The arrangement is alphabetical by city with data covering such topics as children's well being, recycling policies, toxic releases, and a pollen calendar to name a few.—*Pref.*

Statistical Record of the Environment, 1991– ***
This source includes both technical and popular statistical data on national environmental issues taken from governmental and nongovernmental sources. This is the best source for anyone who needs U.S. data at a glance.

World Resources, 1986– (biennial) ***
The World Resources Institute report distills a vast array of environmental information from sources worldwide. The core of the report provides about 50 data tables that describe conditions of the people and environment in 146 countries; these are supplemented by documentary chapters that synthesize the numbers.

World Resources ... A Guide to the Global Environment, 1994/95– ***
This is the World Resources Institute's authoritative database on global conditions and trends, and is an excellent research and reference tool, providing economic, population, natural resource and environmental statistics. World Resources Institute is an

organization funded by the UN, some national governments and private organizations to study the relationship between economic development strategies and environmental issues.

Try more general sources if the resources listed above are not available at your library.
American Statistics Index ***
Statistical Reference Index ***
Index to International Statistics ***
Statistical Universe *** (online version of the above three titles)

Manuals for Action

Listed below are some publications that will be useful for individual activities and for group activities in elementary and middle schools:

Call to Action: Handbook for Ecology, Peace, and Justice. 1990.
The Sierra Club has published this guidebook that suggests actions individuals can take to help revitalize the environment.

Environmental Awareness Activities for Libraries and Teachers; 20 Interdisciplinary Units for Use in Grades 2–8. 1995.
Martha Seif Simpson had the following goals in mind:
- To increase students' awareness of nature and environmental issues,
- To provide an interdisciplinary curriculum for each environmental issue,
- To encourage students to use a variety of current nonfiction sources to research these activities, and
- To encourage students to work together in small groups.

The Animal Rights Handbook; Everyday Ways to Save Animal Lives. 1990.
Many things one needs to know about animal rights issues are in this book such as fur ranching, product testing, and factory farming.

How to Make the World a Better Place: A Guide to Doing Good. 1990.

50 Simple Things Kids Can Do to Save the Earth. 1990.
The focus group is 8- to 12-year olds but many of the projects could easily be used by adults for family projects.

50 Simple Things You Can Do to Save the Earth. 1989.
The Earthworks Group provides solutions and activities that "empower the individual to get up and do something about global environmental problems."—*Introd.*

Worms Eat Our Garbage: Classroom Activities for a Better Environment. 1993.
This is a book of lessons on recycling and composting by way of worms.

Hands-on Exerecises

Two exercises, with all steps in worksheet format, are included in the text at the end of the chapter. The remaining exercises will be found only on the accompanying disk. All of the exercises may be customized to fit the circumstances in individual libraries.

- A patron wants to begin recycling at home and has decided to start with kitchen waste like organic materials like banana peel, egg shells, etc., and yard waste. Where can the patron get information on how to design a backyard bin?

- A patron has received a solicitation in the mail from the Sierra Club Legal Defense Fund. She has been a member of the Sierra Club for a long time and feels she would support any of their works but she wants to find out a bit more about this fund. Where can she find that information?

- A patron needs to write a paper on world fish production. He especially wants to know which countries have the largest fishing fleets. And where does the United States fit in a listing of the world's top fishing nations?

- What is formaldehyde? What are the major sources? What are formaldehyde-related symptoms?

- A patron owns a home that was built at the beginning of the 20th century and is concerned that the paint might contain lead. He wants to read about lead-based paint and what he might have to do before he can sell the house. A related question is about lead-based products and health.

- The Clean Air Act is considered landmark legislation because it set national policy and standards for pollution control. When was it enacted? What amendments have been added and how did they further this line of legislation?

- The settlers of Plymouth Colony were so concerned about lumber resources they enacted early legislation. What was that legislation?

- John and William Bartram were father-and-son naturalists and conducted some of the earliest explorations of the nation.

- Two businessmen have just purchased a property that used to be an automobile repair garage and all the old junk is still on the property. They want to be able to dispose of the materials environmentally, especially the steel metal. Where can they find the name of a company or companies in their area that will deal with that type of environmental debris?

- The EPA has 10 regional offices. Where are they located and what are the telephone numbers?

- A student who is trying to write a research paper on the subject of environmental justice has encountered three concepts—environmental inequalities, environmental racism, and environmental justice. Is there a difference? What laws, treaties, bills, or executive orders deal directly with these issues?

- What are the pros and the cons of government regulation for a cleaner environment? Find at least three readings that project the view that government regulations are necessary for a cleaner environment. Then find three other readings that project the view that government regulations are not necessary for a cleaner environment.

- Locate recycling statistics for countries other than the United States over the past twenty years. Locate comparative statistics on recycling in the United States. What conclusions can you draw when you compare the U.S. with a developed country and a developing country?

- Is the American lifestyle bad for the environment? Use *The Environment; Opposing Viewpoints* to begin the research for this question.

- Overpopulation is not merely a crisis of food, but also of resources, development, deforestation, land mismanagement, and urbanization.

- Many states have enacted legislation regarding various aspects of recycling. Identify the legislation that has been passed in your own state. Identify any agencies that have been created.

- A gentleman at the reference desk is inquiring about the group called Citizens for a Better Environment. He wants to find information about the group. Is there a membership fee? Does it issue any publications?

- An interesting new area that is currently evolving is the use of wetlands (man-made) for wastewater treatment. Are these man-made sites more effective than natural ones?

- Biodiversity is a new exciting area because of its important potential for finding beneficial new drugs. For example, the Rosy Periwinkle (*cantharanthus roseus*) has provided us with two drugs: vinblastine for treatment of Hodgkin's Disease and vincristine for the treatment of leukemia.

- The Endangered Species Act is especially important to environmentalists. What are the implications of the Act?

Environmental Sciences Exercise

A patron wants to begin recycling at home and has decided to start with organic kitchen waste like banana peel, egg shells, etc., and yard waste. Where can the patron get information on how to design a backyard bin?

Use printed and electronic sources as appropriate to answer the reference question.

Step 1   Locate a print resource.

Title of printed source & page numbers:

Step 2   Locate an electronic resource.

Name of the site:

URL:

Step 3   Describe your search strategy.

Environmental Sciences Exercise

A patron needs to write a paper on world fish production. He especially wants to know which countries have the largest fishing fleets. And where does the United States fit in a listing of the world's top fishing nations?

Use printed and electronic sources as appropriate to answer the reference question.

Step 1   Locate a print resource.

Title of printed source & page numbers:

Step 2   Locate an electronic resource.

Name of the site:

URL:

Step 3   Briefly write the answers here.

Step 4   Describe your search strategy.

Genealogy Research Resources

Audrey Abbott Iacone
Reference Librarian
Carnegie Library of Pittsburgh

Introduction

Genealogy is the first cousin of History. The research tools are the same; however, most genealogists are not trained historians and approach this avenue of study with limited or languished library skills. The novice genealogists will be overwhelmed by the myriad resources available to them. The process is complex, it is time consuming, it can become expensive, and patrons may become discouraged.

It is the reference librarian's first duty to see that their patrons are provided with instruction on how to proceed, suggestions for the best resources to consult, and directions on where these resources are located. Basic instruction in the traditional or electronic catalog may also be necessary. It is wise to suggest to your patrons that they read a basic genealogical manual or "how to" book—several are included in the selected genealogy resources—and that they take a course on Beginning Genealogy. Local community colleges and genealogical societies frequently offer these.

Basic resources for genealogists include the census, newspapers, city directories, county and regional histories, maps, cemetery indexes, religious records, wills, deeds, military records, naturalizations, and vital records. Your library may provide biography indexes, clipping files, photograph collections, and family files unique to your library. Genealogists will devour these.

Besides the standard library resources, genealogists will also need to include in their investigation other repositories, courthouses, churches/synagogues, cemeteries, and the Internet. It is important to be able to provide addresses to these agencies and also basic information about their holdings. It is not enough to know your own collection; it is essential to also become familiar with other regional libraries and historical societies.

The Internet provides exciting possibilities for the genealogist, but there are pitfalls. There are hundreds of genealogy related web sites, but many are fee-based, some are information shallow, and many only transitory. Many genealogists believe that the Internet will solve all of their research problems. They believe that if they just type in an ancestor's name, then their pedigree all the way back to Charlemagne will appear on the screen. Of course, this is not the case.

The success of your patron's research may depend upon how effectively you know and understand the genealogical process. You want them to make the most efficient use of their time in your library. It is your job to guide them. Genealogy is searching for the pieces of a large puzzle that extend back through time and across enormous geographic distances. Many pieces will remain lost and there will be obstacles to research. But with guidance, your patrons will be able to begin to successfully locate and assemble the pieces that will complete their family's picture.

Components of the Instruction and Training

- Discuss the genealogical process with the trainees. An outline is included in this chapter that can be used as a class handout for training; it can also be used as a patron pathfinder.
- Discuss searching the library catalog using subject headings. Also discuss how patrons could easily adapt the headings for use as keywords.

Your patrons should begin by studying several **"how to" books**
 Genealogy—Handbooks, manuals, etc.

Search for **family names**
 Abbott family
 Heraldry

Search for materials by **country, state, or county**
 Wales—Genealogy—Handbooks, manuals, etc.
 New York—Genealogy—Handbooks, manuals, etc.
 Salem County (NJ) Genealogy
 Bucks County (PA)—History

Search for materials by **ethnic group**
 Italian Americans—Genealogy—Bibliography
 Polish Americans—Genealogy—Handbooks, manuals, etc.

Other useful subject headings for various types of searches:

For **vital records** such as birth, death, and marriage:
  Registers of births, etc.—Detroit
  Registers of births, etc.—United States
For **web site research**:
  Genealogy—Data processing
For collecting information on a **home computer**:
  Genealogy—Software
For **writing your family history**:
  Bibliographical citations—Handbooks, manuals, etc.
  Genealogy—Authorship
For journals and genealogical **periodicals**:
  Genealogy—Periodicals

The Genealogical Process

Begin with the present

Genealogical research should begin with the present generation and work backward through time. Do not allow your patron to start with a Revolutionary War ancestor or original immigrant. It is too easy to get lost when moving forward through time. That early ancestor may have had ten children and your patron probably won't know from which child he/she is descended. Always begin with today.

Start with what you know

The process begins with you. You know yourself very well. Begin collecting information on yourself - birth record, marriage record, achievements, employment, education. Obtain documents to verify the information. Include photographs to enhance the "picture" of yourself and your family.

Vital Records are...vital

Birth, death, and marriage records are the essential building blocks of any individual's history. If you know **where** and **when** these three events took place, then the other pieces will more easily fall into place. Locating these facts can be challenging. The librarians can best assist their patrons if they know where this information is located.

Vital Records are usually held by state, county, and local governments. These records, especially birth records, may be restricted. It is important to know the dates that government agencies began to maintain their records. For the 20th century, most states record and maintain the birth and death records of their residents. The starting dates differ by state. For Pennsylvania, these records begin in 1906. Before 1906, these records were maintained by the counties but only back to 1870. Before 1870, the researcher may need to search for church and cemetery records.

Marriage Records in Pennsylvania are held by the counties and begin in 1885. If your patron is seeking information about a wedding that took place in Greene County in 1911, then you would suggest that he/she contact the Greene County Courthouse. Sources for marriage dates also include churches, especially for the period before the government began to keep records. If your patron needs information on a wedding that took place in 1862 in Bucks County, then he/she should start searching in that county for possible church records.

Document! Document! Document!

Cite your sources. Teach the difference between primary and secondary sources. For every birth date, provide a birth record or baptismal certificate. For every wedding, provide a marriage record or church certificate. Teach your patrons how to cite their sources. Several books and manuals of style can be used. Remind your patrons that they should be documenting a paper trail that any future relative can follow. For every will, provide the city, county, courthouse, office, will book number, and page number. A hundred years from now, their descendants can visit that same courthouse and locate the will. For books, include title, edition, and page number. Other family members may wish to review that information to seek clues to their particular research.

Continue the process for past generations

Continue with your parents, then your grandparents. You will notice that the number of persons that you are researching increases with every generation: 1 genealogist, 2 parents, 4 grandparents, 8 great - grandparents, 16..., 32..., 64... If you include the siblings for all of these folks, and you should, then the number of ancestors that you are tracking can be enormous.

Organize your records

Keeping all the names, dates, and relationships straight can be overwhelming. Genealogy manuals usually address this issue as well as the dilemma of how to number generations and individuals. The abundance of new software programs offers a solution to this problem. Books are available that discuss the components of these products.

Preserve your documents

Locating information and obtaining photos, certificates, and letters is the first hurdle to overcome. It is then imperative to preserve what you collect. Storage and handling conditions can effect the longevity of the items that you seek to preserve. Temperature, humidity, and housing are important elements to consider. Storing an old newspaper article in an acidic folder in a damp basement is a formula for disaster. It is important to maintain a constant temperature and humidity level and store precious documents in mylar or acid free folders and boxes.

Writing the family history

Provide your patrons with guidebooks that will direct their efforts to bring their research to a final conclusion. Family newsletters provide an excellent way to share research results with living relatives. Compiling the total research into a book format is the best way to preserve their research. Donated copies to local libraries and historical societies will ensure that others in the future will benefit from the author's years of research. Several publications will assist your patrons as they take this final step in the genealogical process.

Note: The Genealogical Process has been included on the accompanying disk so it can easily be reproduced and/or customized for patrons.

Selected Genealogy Research Resources

In this chapter, the resources are arranged in the following categories:
> Bibliographies
> Dictionaries
> Directories
> Ethnic Resources
> Handbooks, Manuals, and Guides
> Passenger and Immigration Lists and Ships
> Titles of Selected Periodicals

Vital Records
Print Resources Regarding Internet Genealogy Resources
Relevant Internet Sites
Writing Family History

Bibliographies

The titles listed below are examples of the various bibliographies that have been compiled. When you are searching for resources within a state, be aware that most state archives have probably published a guide.

American & British Genealogy & Heraldry. 1983 ed.
This is an annotated reference manual for librarians.

A Bibliography of American County Histories. 1987 ed.
This resource identifies county histories of any consequence for all states except Alaska and Hawaii.

Genealogical & Local History Books in Print. 1997.
These volumes contain lists of books, by region, state, county, and municipality. They include the title, author, publisher, number of pages, price, and vendor.

Genealogies Cataloged by the Library of Congress Since 1986: With a List of Established Forms of Family Names and a List of Genealogies Converted to Microform Since 1983. 1992.
This volume lists 8,997 genealogies cataloged by the Library of Congress between 1986 and 1991. This includes an index by surname and one by author. There is also a surname list taken from the Library's database of authorized subject headings. Finally, there is also a list of older genealogies that have been replaced with microfilm copies.

Reference Sources for Canadian Genealogy. 1995.
Name, title, and subject indexes are included.

Dictionaries

Concise Genealogical Dictionary. 1989.
Definitions are provided for unfamiliar words encountered in the process of researching one's family.

A Dictionary of Surnames. 1988.
European names, definitions, variations, linguistic origins, and current distributions are listed.

The Oxford Companion to Local and Family History. 1996.
Over 2,000 entries cover fields such as social, agricultural, and family history in the British Isles. An Appendix lists national and major county record offices in England, Scotland, and Wales.

Directories

The Ancestry Family Historian's Address Book. 1998.
This is a comprehensive list of local, state, and federal agencies, institutions, ethnic, and genealogical organizations.

Cemeteries of the U.S.: A Guide to Contact Information for U.S. Cemeteries and Their Records. 1994.
Many genealogists will be looking for information about cemeteries.

County Courthouse Book. 1996 ed.
This is a directory of courthouses in the United States.

Directory of Family Associations. 1996 ed.
Individuals and groups who have formed associations around a common ancestor or family name are listed. These groups frequently publish newsletters.

The Genealogist's Address Book. 1995 ed.
The listings include national and state organizations, ethnic and religious organizations, archives, libraries, historical and genealogical societies, hereditary societies, adoption registries, immigration research centers, publishers, among others.

The State & Province Vital Records Guide. 1993.
This directory leads the genealogist to the place of birth, death, and marriage, and divorce certificates in the United States, U.S. insular areas and territories, and Canada.

Ethnic Resources

There are dozens of titles that apply to various ethnic groups. The list of titles below is simply a sampling to give you an idea of the range. Search your catalog by keyword using the name of the ethnic group or country of origin and the word genealogy—perhaps truncated.

Asian American Genealogical Sourcebook. 1995.
The Encyclopedia of Jewish Genealogy, 1991–
Discovering Your Italian Ancestors: How to Find and Record Your Unique Heritage. 1997.
The Family Tree Detective: Tracing Your Ancestors in England and Wales. 1997 ed.
Guide to Cuban Genealogical Research: Records and Sources. 1991.
Hispanic American Genealogical Sourcebook. 1995.
In Search of Your German Roots. 1994 ed.
Native American Genealogical Sourcebook. 1995.
Polish Roots. 1993.
Sources for Research in English Genealogy. 1989.
Sources for Research in Scottish Genealogy. 1992.
A Student's Guide to African American Genealogy. 1996
A Student's Guide to Scandinavian American Genealogy. 1996.
Tracing Your Irish Ancestors: The Complete Guide. 1992.

Handbooks, Manuals, & Guides

The Genealogist's Companion & Sourcebook. 1994.
"A beyond-the-basics, hands-on guide to unpuzzling your past."—*Cover.*

Guide to Genealogical Research in the National Archives. 1985.
Arranged by Record Groups, this source provides information on those materials most frequently used by genealogists. It includes the census, passenger arrival lists, naturalization records, military records, and records of Native Americans.

Guide to Naturalization Records of the United States. 1997.
This guide is arranged by state and then by county. If records have been filmed, the film number is supplied. Each state chapter includes a list of genealogical resources which pertains to that state. An appendix includes Native American records.

The Handy Book for Genealogists: United States of America. 1994 ed.
Provides information on each state including a brief history, the state capital, dates of statehood, and color maps. There is a special section on migratory routes. There are also lists of genealogical archives, libraries, and societies. The holdings of county courthouses are supplied.

The Librarian's Genealogy Notebook: A Guide to Resources. 1998.
This handbook by Dahrl Elizabeth Moore is a publication of the American Library Association. The author shows librarians how to maximize resources in their libraries, how to obtain information from external sources, and includes general sources which libraries may want to provide access or own.

Obituaries: A Guide to Sources. 1992 ed.
The author has identified about 3,500 books, articles, and periodicals that provide or lead to obituary information. One section deals with international sources. The indexing is by names of counties or towns as well as by titles of the periodicals.

The Researchers Guide to American Genealogy. 1988 ed.
This is probably the definitive, all-purpose reference guide for genealogists.

Unpuzzling Your Past: A Basic Guide to Genealogy. 1995 ed.
This handbook by Emily Anne Croom is an excellent guide for novice genealogists. Useful charts and forms are provided for organizing the various family lines.

Passenger and Immigration Lists and Ships

Czech Immigration Passenger Lists. 1983.
The Famine Immigrants: Lists of Irish Immigrants Arriving at the Port of New York, 1846-1851. 1983.
Germans to America: Lists of Passengers Arriving at U.S. Ports, 1850– . 1988–
Italians to America: Lists of Passengers Arriving at U.S. Ports, 1880-1899, 1992–

Passenger and Immigration Lists Bibliography, 1538–1900. 1981.
This resource suggests articles and books that provide the researcher with documentation for numerous ships arriving in North America.

Passenger and Immigration Lists Index: A Guide to Published Arrival Records of about 500,000 passengers Who Came to the United States and Canada in the Seventeenth, Eighteenth, and Nineteenth Centuries, 1981–
This multi-volume set provides researchers with an extensive list of names that covers all ports, all nationality groups, and all time periods.

Ships of Our Ancestors. 1993 ed.
Pictures of hundreds of sailing ships and steamships are contained in this title.

They Came in Ships: A Guide to Finding Your Immigrant Ancestor's Arrival Record. 1993.
Step-by-step directions on how to identify your ancestor's ship are provided as well as where to locate the passenger arrival records.

Titles of Selected Periodicals

The American Genealogist
Genealogical Helper
Heritage Quest
National Genealogical Society Quarterly
New England Historical and Genealogical Register
The New York Genealogical and Historical Record
The Pennsylvania Genealogical Magazine
The Virginia Genealogist

Vital Records

International Vital Records Handbook. 1988.
This handbook provides addresses and forms to request birth, death, and marriage records in other countries.

The State and Province Vital Records Guide. 1993.
This directory leads the genealogist to the place to order birth, death, marriage, and divorce certificates in the United States, U.S. insular areas and territories, and Canada.

Vital Records Handbook. 1990.
Addresses and forms to request birth, death, and marriage records are provided for all states in the U.S.

Print Resources Regarding Internet Genealogy Sites

Genealogy Online: Researching Your Roots. 1998.
"Guidance for genealogists at all levels-beginning, intermediate, and advanced."—*Cover.*

The Internet for Genealogists: A Beginner's Guide. 1997 ed.
This guide introduces the Internet and provides a list of genealogical resources.

Netting Your Ancestors: Genealogical Research on the Internet. 1997
This book by Cyndi Howells, the creator of *Cyndi's List of Genealogical Sites on the Internet*, is a basic guide to accessing the Internet with separate chapters on Mailing Lists and Newsgroups and E-mail.

Virtual Roots: A Guide to Genealogy and Local History on the World Wide Web. 1997.
This books lists genealogy and local history web sites from around the world. It includes a section on Family Associations.

Relevant Internet Sites

Cyndi's List of Genealogy Sites on the Internet
http://www.CyndisList.com/
One of the largest and best organized sites for genealogy links. *Cindi's* has more than 90 categories which she constantly monitors and updates.

Ancestry's Maps and Gazetteers
http://www.ancestry.com/ancestry/maps.asp
This site provides access to dozens of historical U.S. and European maps and gazetteers.

ROOTS-L Home Page
http://www.rootsweb.com/roots-l/
This mailing list is presently the largest genealogical mailing list. Use this site to locate others researching the same family names.

Social Security Death Index
http://www.ancestry.com/ssdi/advanced.htm
The *SSDI* provides information about 40 million persons who have died between 1937 and 1994. The index may provide birth and death dates, last place of residence, state where person was issued a Social Security Number, and the Social Security Number. Information from the index can then be used to obtain further information from the Social Security Administration.

Library of Congress
http://lcweb.loc.gov/
The user may research the catalogs of the Library of Congress and other libraries. Here you will find a rich source of genealogical and local history resources.

This site is provided by a group of volunteers for genealogical research in every state and in every county of the U.S. Researchers can post queries, search a Surname Index, check on family reunions, and locate information on Civil War Regiments.

Writing the Family History

Cite Your Sources: A Manual for Documenting Family Histories and Genealogical Records. 1980.
This manual clearly explains how to cite genealogical documents such as wills, census records, and family Bibles.

Evidence! 1997.
This is the latest comprehensive source for citing genealogical evidence.

Writing Family Histories and Memoirs. 1995.
This is a guide to organizing and writing the history of your family.

Your Family History: A Handbook for Research and Writing. 1986.
Summary data sheets to compile information about each family member are provided, along with examples of compelling family stories.

Hands-on Exercises

Eleven exercises have been listed. The first six have detailed research strategies and steps worked out and have been set up on worksheets for the user. No strategies have been developed for the remaining five. They are listed simply to give the instructor some additional ideas for exercises. All of the exercises may be customized to fit the circumstances in individual libraries and their researchers.

- **The patron is searching for an obituary, but does not have the exact date of death.**
  Obituaries or death notices can vary in length depending on the time period, the newspaper, and the social prominence of the deceased. It is important to remember that a death notice or obituary was not always published and thus may never be found Sometimes, during periods of epidemics when large numbers of persons died, not everyone's name found its way into the newspaper.

- **A patron is trying to locate an ancestor in the Census.**
  The census was taken every ten years beginning in 1790. The most recent census to which we have access is 1920. The 1890 census was almost completely destroyed by fire; fragments are available. There are printed indexes for most states for every

census year. Beginning in 1880, the index is called a Soundex and is available on microfilm. The census itself is also available on microfilm.

Keep in mind that indexes are incomplete, spelling variations abound, the handwriting could be illegible, and the census enumerator rarely asked "How do you spell your name?"

- **The researcher wishes to locate a naturalization record.**
  Naturalization was a voluntary process and not required. In the 18th and 19th centuries, an immigrant could have been naturalized in any court in the country – county, state, federal, and mayor's courts. Beginning in 1907, the federal government standardized the process.

  To be naturalized is a three-step process. First comes the Declaration of Intent, then the Petition for Naturalization, and finally the actual document granting Citizenship or Naturalization. Sometimes this final document is still in the family's possession; it can help to locate the first two documents by identifying the appropriate court.

- **The genealogist is searching for information about the immigrant ancestor's port and date of arrival and the name of the ship.**
  Sometimes a researcher already knows the three key elements in locating ship passenger information. Sometimes they only have one or two of these important facts.

  Passenger Indexes to major ports and to some minor ports exist. These and lists of passengers by ship and by port are available on microfilm in many libraries or can be obtained from commercial lenders. They are also available at the National Archives and its branches.

- **The patron's ancestor died in Iowa, but was born in Pennsylvania in 1804. He doesn't know where the ancestor was born or the name of the parents.**

- **The patron is searching for a Marriage Record in Pennsylvania in 1852.**
  Vital Records are essential to any accurate genealogical search. No family history is complete without birth, death, and marriage records. For the 20th century, these records are usually easy to acquire. They are collected and maintained by states and counties. In Pennsylvania, birth and death records are maintained by the state beginning in 1906. Some counties have these records from 1870–1905. Counties have marriage records beginning in 1885.

As the researcher moves back in time, these records become harder to locate. Churches and cemeteries are the best sources of information. The census can also provide helpful clues.

Suggestions for further exercises:
- The patron is searching for the maiden name of her grandmother.
- The researcher needs to locate the home village of his ancestor in Ireland.
- The genealogist seeks to confirm the names of the siblings of his grandfather.
- The patron needs the address of an uncle who lived in Pittsburgh in 1940.
- The patron was adopted and seeks to identify and to locate his natural parents.

NAME...

Genealogy Exercise

The patron is searching for an obituary, but does not have the exact date of death.

Obituaries or death notices can vary in length depending on the time period, the newspaper, and the social prominence of the deceased. It is important to remember that a death notice or obituary was not always published and thus may never be found Sometimes, during periods of epidemics when large numbers of persons died, not everyone's name found its way into the newspaper.

Step 1   If the patron has a close approximate date of death, then he can scan several weeks worth of newspapers. Older newspapers do not supply a front page key indicating on what page the obituaries, death rolls, or necrologies are located. Called by various names and sometimes listed in several places in the newspapers, they can be hard to find.

Step 2   Perhaps your library has produced an Index to Death Notices. This can save a great deal of time. Once a date of death is located, then the patron should search through all available newspapers. Local newspapers in small communities frequently wrote larger pieces than can be found in the newspapers of bigger cities and thus provide the researcher with more detail on the ancestor's life.

Step 3   If the patron has a real idea of the date of death, then he should contact the cemetery where the deceased is buried. This always is a good idea anyway because cemetery records and tombstones may include other information on the deceased. The records may also indicate if other members of the same family are buried there. Cemetery records may only provide the date of interment, but that is usually enough to locate the obituary.

Step 4   The patron does not know where the ancestor is buried. Use census records and city directories to locate where the deceased was living. People are often buried near where they lived. Religious and ethnic clues will help to further determine which cemeteries are the most likely to investigate further.

Step 5   State Departments of Vital Records will often conduct a multiple year search for a Death Record for a fee. Provide the address and encourage the patron to try this avenue of investigation. In any case, once the exact date of death is established, the patron will want to obtain the Death Record.

Genealogy Exercise

A patron is trying to locate an ancestor in the Census.

The census was taken every ten years beginning in 1790. The most recent census to which we have access is 1920. The 1890 census was almost completely destroyed by fire; fragments are available. There are printed indexes for most states for every census year. Beginning in 1880, the index is called a Soundex and is available on microfilm. The census itself is also available on microfilm.

Keep in mind that indexes are incomplete, spelling variations abound, the handwriting could be illegible, and the census enumerator rarely asked "How do you spell your name?"

Step 1   You must ask the patron a series of questions:

In what time period are you interested? Where did the ancestor live? What state? Do you know the county? Do you know the township or ward?

Step 2   Depending on the answers to these questions, you will refer the patron to the appropriate indexes.

Step 3   The patron searches the indexes, but does not find the surname he/she is seeking.

Remind the patron to check other regional volumes for the state. The ancestor may have lived in the East, West, Central, North, or South of the state.

Step 4   If the patron searches all available indexes and spelling variations, does not find the name he is seeking, but he knows exactly where the ancestor lived, then he can go directory into the census and search any township or ward page by page until he finds the ancestral family.

Step 5   What other sources can help a researcher to determine exactly where an ancestor lived?

Consider having the researcher check for property deeds and/or city directories.

Genealogy Exercise

The researcher wishes to locate a naturalization record.

Naturalization was a voluntary process and not required. In the 18th and 19th centuries, an immigrant could have been naturalized in any court in the country – county, state, federal, and mayor's courts. Beginning in 1907, the federal government standardized the process.

To be naturalized is a three-step process. First comes the Declaration of Intent, then the Petition for Naturalization, and finally the actual document granting Citizenship or Naturalization. Sometimes this final document is still in the family's possession; it can help to locate the first two documents by identifying the appropriate court.

Step 1   Ask the patron if his family has the original Citizenship paper presented to the immigrant when he was granted his naturalization. With the court identified, then the patron can write to the designated court and request copies of the first two documents. Frequently, however, the first two documents no longer exist or can't be found, only indexes remain.

Step 2   The patron does not have the final document. Ask where the original immigrant entered the country. Did the immigrant tarry there for a while? The patron should begin his search in the county where the immigrant stayed.

Step 3   The immigrant may have begun the process in one place and continued it in another. The patron should search in the county or counties where the immigrant ultimately settled.

Step 4   The immigrant may have begun the process, but never completed it. The immigrant may have **never** been naturalized; it was **not** required. How do you know?

Have the researcher search the 1900, 1910, and 1920 censuses. These ask questions about the status of a person's citizenship and if naturalized, in what year.

NAME...

Genealogy Exercise

The genealogist is searching for information about the immigrant ancestor's port and date of arrival and the name of the ship.

Sometimes a researcher already knows the three key elements in locating ship passenger information. Sometimes they only have one or two of these important facts.

Passenger Indexes to major ports and to some minor ports exist. These and lists of passengers by ship and by port are available on microfilm in many libraries or can be obtained from commercial lenders. They are also available at the National Archives and its branches.

Step 1   The researcher knows nothing about his immigrant ancestor's arrival. Ask if he has searched for Naturalization information. This may be very useful. Port of arrival, ship's name, and arrival date can be listed on the Declaration of Intent and the Petition for Naturalization.

Step 2   Have the patron check the available indexes to the major ports. Sometimes you must make an educated guess as to the correct port. If an immigrant settled in Pennsylvania, then the three most likely ports to search are Philadelphia, Baltimore, and New York.

Step 3   The patron knows the port and the date, but not the name of the ship. The patron can still consult the indexes and/or the passenger lists. The patron can also search in the *Morton Allan Directory of European Passenger Steamship Arrivals* (1890–1930). There you will find the name of the ship, then the patron can bypass the indexes and begin to search in the actual passenger lists.

Step 4   The ancestor arrived in New York in 1875. The index to New York does not cover 1847–1896. There are printed passenger indexes by nationality such as *Germans to America* and *Italians to America*. The early part of the *Morton Allan Directory* may help for 1890–1896.

Step 5   The ancestor arrived in Colonial America before passenger lists were common. There are numerous books, articles, and web sites that provide information on early passengers. There is also the series plus supplements entitled *Passenger and Immigration Lists Index*. These books cover all time periods, all ports, and all nationalities.

Genealogy Exercise

The patron's ancestor died in Iowa, but was born in Pennsylvania in 1804. He doesn't know where the ancestor was born or the name of the parents.

Step 1   The patron needs to discover when the ancestor arrived in Iowa. Was it as a young child or as an adult? The patron should search Iowa census indexes to see when the name first appears. Someone with the last name may be the ancestor's father.

Step 2   The patron could also search the Pennsylvania census indexes for 1800 and 1810 looking for anyone with that particular surname. This works best if the surname is unusual.

If the surname is located, then the patron should begin to search in county histories for family information. There should also be a search of property deeds and wills in that county. Perhaps someone with the same last name sold property in Union County in 1811 and moved to Iowa. Perhaps someone with the same last name died in Erie County and left money to the ancestor in Iowa. These could be relatives or even parents.

Step 3   If the census index search is not helpful, the patron should exhaust all resources in Iowa. What do county and township histories say about the origins of the earliest settlers? Do church or cemetery records reveal anything? Property Deeds may identify the previous residence of the buyer. Did the ancestor buy or inherit property from someone with the same last name? Find any obituaries or death notices in local Iowa newspapers.

Step 4   If the ancestor belonged to a particular ethnic or religious group, then the patron should search for information about that group's emigration patterns. For instance if the ancestor were a Quaker, the patron may discover that a group of Quakers from Fayette County, PA traveled West in 1825 to settle in Iowa. This could be useful information and would direct the search to a particular county in Pennsylvania.

Genealogy Exercise

The patron is searching for a Marriage Record in Pennsylvania in 1852.

Vital Records are essential to any accurate genealogical search. No family history is complete without birth, death, and marriage records. For the 20th century, these records are usually easy to acquire. They are collected and maintained by states and counties. In Pennsylvania, birth and death records are maintained by the state beginning in 1906. Some counties have these records from 1870–1905. Counties have marriage records beginning in 1885.

As the researcher moves back in time, these records become harder to locate. Churches and cemeteries are the best sources of information. The census can also provide helpful clues.

Step 1   The first fact to establish is the place of the wedding. Does the patron know the county or the township where the marriage took place?

Step 2   The next item to determine is the religion of the couple. Were they Roman Catholic or Baptist? This will help to narrow down the list of possible choices of churches in any given township.

Step 3   Use city directories and published county histories to determine what churches existed in a particular place and where they were located.

Step 4   Tracking down elusive church records can be frustrating. The original church may no longer exist. Did the records follow the parishioners to the new church? Did the records end up in a repository for that particular denomination? Are they accessible? Indexed? Did the records travel with the minister or priest to his new church? Did the records burn with the old church building?

Step 5   For a brief period in Pennsylvania, 1852–55, some vital records were being recorded in each county. These records and their indexes are available on microfilm. Although not complete, they can be of immense use to researchers. Other states may have similar pockets of records in existence. Some states have records that go back quite far into the 19th century.

Step 6   Finally, your library may have produced an index to Marriage Notices in local newspapers. Such an index would be useful although it may not be complete.

Federal Legislative Research on the Web

THOMAS M. TWISS

Public Services Librarian
THE COLLEGE OF NEW JERSEY

Introduction

"I have to trace the history of a bill. Can you help me get started?"
"I recently heard about a bill that is before Congress. How can I get a copy?"
"Could you tell me who my legislator is and how I can contact him or her?"

These are just a few of the questions related to U.S. federal legislation that are frequently heard at the reference desk. In the past, most legislative questions could only be answered in a federal depository library equipped with a variety of indexes and housing an extensive collection of government documents in print, microfilm, and microfiche. Today, a large percentage of legislative questions can be answered easily in many small libraries and homes by consulting the World Wide Web.

This chapter deals with legislative questions frequently encountered in libraries. It is designed especially for small college or public libraries that are not federal depositories. For that reason, it does not deal with traditional print resources found mainly in depositories. Nor does it deal with many useful but expensive commercial services that provide legislative information via the Web. The resources discussed are all legislative Web sites that can be accessed for free.

Most legislative questions that can be answered using the Web can be answered with a number of different Web resources. However, for this chapter it was necessary to limit the sites examined for each question to one or a few. The Web sites included here were selected because they tend to be well established, they provide the most extensive coverage and information, and they offer the easiest searching and/or the largest number of search options. *THOMAS* (the Library of Congress's legislative site) and *GPO Access* (the site of the Government Printing Office) meet these criteria most frequently.

It is important to remember that anything on the Web can change very quickly. Consequently, the information included in this chapter should be checked carefully before any actual instruction session.

The Legislative Process and the Trail of Documents

Federal legislative research requires a clear understanding of the major steps in the legislative process and the types of documents generated at each stage. This is true whether the researcher is writing a legislative history, attempting to find the current status of a bill, looking for a specific legislative document, or trying to evaluate a legislator's voting record. The most important steps and documents in the legislative process are as follows:

1. The bill is introduced on the floor of the House or Senate. It is assigned to one or more committees.
   Documents: Bills are published by the Government Printing Office. The reading of bill titles, the names of bill sponsors, and the referral of bills to committees are reported daily in the *Congressional Record*.

2. A committee usually refers the bill to one or more subcommittees. Committees and subcommittees often hold public hearings that provide an opportunity for experts and interested parties to testify about the merits of a proposed piece of legislation. Also, committees may commission studies related to a particular bill.
   Documents: Committee hearings are frequently, but not always, published. Studies commissioned by committees are sometimes published as committee prints.

3. A committee may amend a bill, approve it, reject it, or simply let it die. If it approves the bill, the committee issues a report to the House or Senate.
   Documents: Reports from a committee, usually recommending the passage of a bill, are published as committee reports.

4. The bill is debated on the floor of the House or Senate. Amendments may also be introduced. At the conclusion of the debate, the bill is voted upon.
   Documents: The debate on the floor of the House and Senate, together with amendments introduced and the final vote, are recorded in the *Congressional Record*.

5. If the bill passes in one chamber of Congress, it is referred to the other chamber for consideration. There, it may repeat all of the previous steps.

6. Often, differing versions of a bill are passed by the House and Senate. When this happens, a conference committee consisting of members of both houses meets to work out the differences. The compromise version is then sent back to both chambers for approval.
   Documents: Conference reports, like committee reports, are published. The final vote on the revised bill is reported in the *Congressional Record*.

7. When the bill is sent to the White House, the president may sign it, veto it, or choose not to act. If the president does not act, the bill automatically becomes law after ten days unless Congress adjourns during that period. In the latter case, the bill simply dies on the president's desk. Congress can override a presidential veto by a two-thirds majority vote in both houses.
   Documents: When signing or vetoing a bill, the president usually makes a statement. These statements are published in a number of different sources. In paper, they are published in the *Weekly Compilation of Presidential Documents* and ultimately in the

The Legislative Process

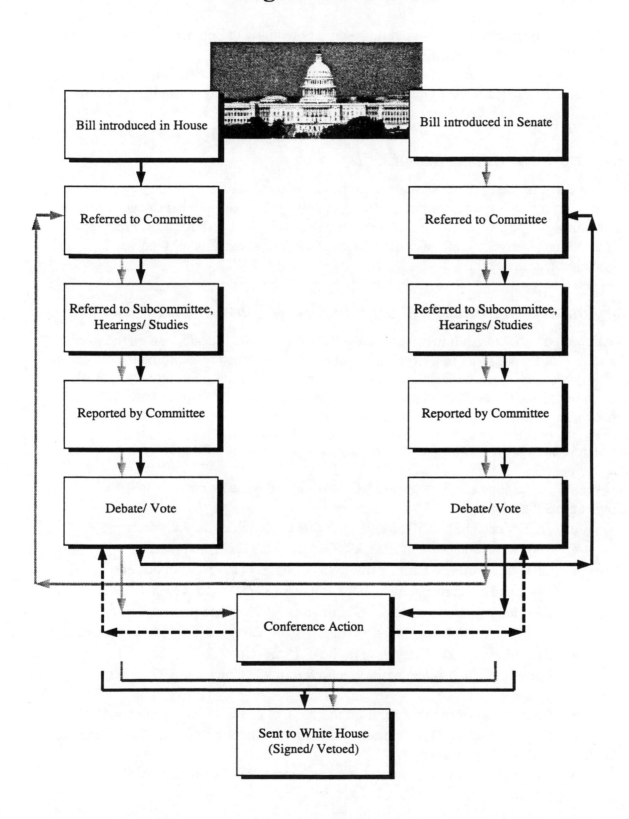

Bill introduced in House

Bill introduced in Senate

Referred to Committee

Referred to Committee

Referred to Subcommittee, Hearings/ Studies

Referred to Subcommittee, Hearings/ Studies

Reported by Committee

Reported by Committee

Debate/ Vote

Debate/ Vote

Conference Action

Sent to White House (Signed/ Vetoed)

Public Papers of the Presidents. Also, they may be published as House or Senate documents that later appear in the *Serial Set*; and they may appear in the *Congressional Record.*

8. The final product is a law—a public law if it potentially affects all citizens, a private law if it affects only specific individuals or organizations.
    Documents: In paper, the law is first published as a slip law. Slip laws are later republished in the *United States Statutes at Large.* Ultimately, all public laws are codified in the *United States Code.*

Finding Information about Bills

Patrons often request information about proposed or past legislation. One frequent assignment for college classes in social work, public policy, or political science is to trace the history of a particular bill. Library patrons also sometimes ask for a summary of a bill under consideration, for the current status of a bill, and for a list of who voted for and who voted against a bill.

Legislative Histories, Bill Summaries, & Current Status of Bills

Writing the history of a bill involves tracing the path from its introduction on the floor of the House or Senate to its final signing by the President. When researching the history of a bill, it is always a good idea to check first to see if someone else has already compiled a legislative history. Legislative histories, bill summaries, and the current status of bills are most easily found on the Library of Congress's *THOMAS.*
(See also the chapter, "Social Welfare Policy: Teaching How To Research a Policy, by Cathy Seitz Whitaker in *Empowering Students; Hands-on Library Instruction Activities,* 1996.)

Source: "Bill Summary & Status" on *THOMAS*—http://thomas.loc.gov/
Coverage: 93rd Congress (1973/74) to present
Information: For each bill, "Bill Summary & Status" provides the following:
  * Sponsor(s) and cosponsor(s), 93rd Congress (1973/74) to present
  * Official, short, and popular titles, 93rd Congress (1973/74) to present
  * Floor and executive actions, 93rd Congress (1973/74) to present
  * Detailed legislative history, 96th Congress (1979/80) to present
  * *Congressional Record* page references, 103rd Congress (1993/94) to present
  * Bill summary, 93rd Congress (1973/74) to present
  * Committees and subcommittees of referral, 93rd Congress (1973/74) to present)
  * Committees of reporting and origin, 96th Congress (1979/80) to present
  * Links to additional committee information including hearings, 104th Congress (1995/96) to present
  * Amendment descriptions and sometimes text, 95th Congress (1975/76) to present

- Subjects (indexing terms assigned to a bill) 93rd Congress (1973/74) to present
- Full text versions of the bill, 103rd Congress (1993/94) to present
- Full text of legislation if the bill was enacted, 101st Congress (1989/90) to present
- Abstracts of legislation, 94th Congress (1975/76) to 102nd Congress (1991/92)
- For laws receiving line-item veto, text of cancellation notices or disapproval, 105th Congress (1997/98) to present

Access: On the *THOMAS* homepage under "Bills," select "Bill Summary and Status: 105th [or current Congress]." Or select "Bill Summary and Status: Previous Congresses" and then select the Congress you want to search. You can search by word or phrase, subject (index term), bill/amendment number, stage in the legislative process, dates of introduction or of floor action, sponsor or cosponsor, committee, or a combination of these. It is also possible to get "Bill Summary & Status" information from lists of all legislation, public laws, and vetoed bills for each Congress.

Help: For additional help in searching "Bill Summary & Status," go to the "Bill Summary & Status" search page for any Congress and select one of the following links under "Help" near the top of the page: "About Bill Summary & Status," "Basic Search," "Advanced Search," or "Interpreting Search Results."

Alternative source: Information on legislative history can also be found in "History of Bills" on *GPO Access*—http://www.access.gpo.gov/su_docs/aces/aaces200.html. This is an electronic version of the "History of Bills and Resolutions" section of the *Congressional Record Index*. Years covered include 1983 to the present.

Who voted for a bill?

This information is not available for all bills since not all bills have recorded or roll call votes. Finding the detailed outcome of a roll call is easiest if you know the roll number, or at least the bill title and/or bill number and the approximate date on which the vote occurred. (If you do not have this information, first try searching "Bill Summary and Status" on *THOMAS* as described above.)

Source: "House Roll Call Votes" on *THOMAS*—http://thomas.loc.gov/. (Note: When you select "House Roll Call Votes" on *THOMAS* you are connected to a server in the House.)
Coverage: 101st Congress, second session (1990) to present
Information: For all roll call votes in the House, the final result, vote totals by party, and an alphabetical list of members for each vote category (yea, nay, present, not voting) are included.
Access: From the *THOMAS* homepage, under "Bills: House Roll Call Votes" select a session of the current Congress, or select "Previous Congresses," then select the session you want to search. Roll call votes are listed in reverse chronological order for each session with roll number, date, issue (bill number), question (description of issue voted upon), vote result, and bill title/description. Click on the link for the appropriate roll number.
Help: From the *THOMAS* homepage, under "Bills: House Roll Call Votes," select "Help."

Source: "Senate Roll Call Votes" on *THOMAS*—http://thomas.loc.gov/. (Note: When you select "Senate Roll Call Votes" on *THOMAS* you are connected to a server in the Senate.)

Coverage: 101ˢᵗ Congress, first session (1989) to present

Information: For all roll call votes in the Senate, the vote result, an alphabetical list of all senators, and an alphabetical list of senators for each vote category (yea, nay, present, not voting) are included.

Access: From the *THOMAS* homepage, under "Bills: Senate Roll Call Votes," select a session of the current Congress, or select "Previous Congresses," then select the session you want to search. Roll call votes are listed in reverse chronological order for each session with roll number, date, bill (number), question (description of issue voted upon), vote result, and bill title/description.

Help: From the *THOMAS* homepage, under "Bills: Senate Roll Call Votes," select "Help."

Finding Congressional Documents

Patrons may ask for specific Congressional documents for a variety of reasons. Sometimes they are writing the history of a bill and want all the relevant legislative documents. In such cases, they should begin by searching for legislative histories as described above or by consulting other sources, including legislative indexes. However, sometimes patrons are looking for a specific document to complete their research. Or, they may be looking for a congressional debate, hearing, or report, or a presidential statement which they have heard about.

Bills

The four types of federal legislation are bills, resolutions, joint resolutions, and concurrent resolutions. The most common and generally most significant are bills.

Source: "Bill Text" on *THOMAS*—http://thomas.loc.gov/

Coverage: 101ˢᵗ Congress (1989/90) to present

Information: The full text of all available versions of bills. Text and, since the 103ʳᵈ Congress (1993/94), PDF versions of bills are available. (Text versions do not look precisely like the original paper version, but they can be downloaded as plain text files and edited in word processing programs. PDF files look exactly like the originals, but cannot be edited with word processing programs.)

Access: *THOMAS* offers three main methods for searching for the full text of bills:

- The fastest way to search for bills from the current Congress is to do a "Quick Search" by entering either the bill number or a word or phrase from the text of the legislation in a box on the left column of the *THOMAS* homepage.
- The second method allows you to locate bills from previous Congresses and provides a number of additional search options. Under "Bills: Billtext:" select the Congress you wish to search. Then enter the word or phrase you want to appear in the bills retrieved, or enter the number of the bill you want to find. You can also choose to limit bills retrieved to bills with floor action (procedural action taken during

consideration of the bill on the floor of the House or Senate), enrolled bills (bills passed by both House and Senate and sent to the President), House bills only, or Senate bills only.

- Finally, the full text of bills introduced in the 103rd Congress or since can be obtained through a "Bill Summary & Status" search (see above). This method provides the greatest number of search options.

Help: For additional help in searching for the full text of bills in *THOMAS*, go to the top of the "Bill Text" search page for any Congress and, under "Help," select "About Bill Text"—http://thomas.loc.gov/home/about.searching.html, or "Searching by Word/phrase"—http://thomas.loc.gov/home/words.html.

Alternative source: "Congressional Bills" on *GPO Access*—http://www.access.gpo.gov/congress/cong009.html—provides all published versions of bills since the 103rd Congress (1993–94).

Congressional Record

The *Congressional Record* is an official record or transcript of the proceedings and debates that occur on the floor of Congress. It is not an exact record of proceedings and debates, since it includes inserted materials and grammatical corrections. It is published daily when Congress is in session.

Source: "*Congressional Record* Text" on *THOMAS*—http://thomas.loc.gov/
Coverage: 101st Congress (1989–90) to present
Information: The full text of *Congressional Record* (including House, Senate, Extensions of Remarks, and Daily Digest) is included.
Access: Three main options are provided for searching the *Congressional Record*:

- For full text of this year's issues, on the *THOMAS* homepage under "*Congressional Record: Congressional Record* Text:" select "Most Recent Issue." Then select the date and section you want to view.
- On the *THOMAS* homepage under "*Congressional Record: Congressional Record* Text:" select a Congress. Then search for a word or phrase or member of the House or Senate, and/or select the date of an issue you want to view. You can also limit your search to the Senate, House, or Extensions of Remarks sections of the *Congressional Record*.
- Since the 103rd Congress, 2nd session (1994), it is possible to search the *Congressional Record Index* that contains links to text in the *Congressional Record*. The *Congressional Record Index* can be searched by word/phrase, or by browsing a list of topics. On the *THOMAS* homepage, under "*Congressional Record: Congressional Record Index*:" select the Congress and session you want to search.

Help: For help in searching the *Congressional Record* in *THOMAS*, see "Searching the *Congressional Record*"—http://thomas.loc.gov/home/search_cr.html.

Alternative source: *"Congressional Record"* on *GPO Access*—
http://www.access.gpo.gov/su_docs/aces/aces150.html—provides the text of the
Congressional Record since the 103rd Congress, second session (1994).

Hearings

Congressional committees hold hearings for a variety of reasons. One of these is to
gather information regarding a proposed piece of legislation. At a hearing, experts and
interested parties present testimony to the members of Congress. Consequently,
published hearings are a good source of information for finding out the views of interest
groups, and for discovering the important concerns surrounding a bill or other
controversial issue. Hearings are often, but not always, published. At this point only a
limited number of hearings are available for free on the Web.

Source: *THOMAS*—http://thomas.loc.gov/. Currently, all hearings accessed through
THOMAS are on House or Senate servers.
Coverage: Selected hearings from the last few years (at the time of this writing, 1995–
1998).
Information: The full text of some testimony. Some committees provide both text and
PDF files. Some committees have no hearings posted.
Access: From the *THOMAS* homepage:
- Under "Committee Information: Committee Home Pages:" select "House" or
  "Senate." Then choose the name of the committee, and select "Hearings" to get a list
  of hearings.
- Or, under "Committee Information: House Committees," choose "Selected Hearing
  Transcripts," then select the committee name, and the hearing. This is faster, but at
  this point fewer hearings options are provided, and no Senate hearings are available
  through this route.

Source: *GPO Access*—http://www.access.gpo.gov/
Coverage: Selected hearings and/or testimony since the 104th Congress, first session
(1995)
Information: Full text of some hearings and/or testimony in text and/or PDF files.
Again, not all committees have made their hearings available on the Web.
Access:
- On the "Congressional Hearings" page—
  http://www.access.gpo.gov/congress/cong017.html—search by word/phrase for 1997
  hearings.
- Or, on the "United States Congress" page—
  http://www.access.gpo.gov/congress/index.html—select "House Committees" or "Senate
  Committees," then the committee, and then (under "Publications"), hearings.
Help: General guidance for searching *GPO Access* is available at "Searching Databases
Online via *GPO Access*"—http://www.access.gpo.gov/su_docs/aces/aces180.shtml.

Alternative sources:

- "Congressional Hearings on the Web," The University of Michigan Documents Center—http://www.lib.umich.edu/libhome/Documents.center/hearings.html—provides access to hearings listed by committee, by government agency testifying, and by lobby group testifying. Also, it provides links for subject indexes of hearings.
- "The U.S. House of Representatives Internet Law Library: Hearings of Congressional Committees"—http://law.house.gov/10.htm—provides access to selected House and Senate hearings listed by committee.

Committee Prints

Committee prints are issued by committees as part of their legislative or oversight functions. Often, they contain reports or studies commissioned by a committee regarding a proposed piece of legislation. Like hearings, they provide a of wealth of information on a wide variety of topics. At this time, committee prints are not available free on the Web.

Committee Reports

Most committee reports contain committee recommendations to the House or Senate regarding a bill. In addition to a summary of the bill and the opinion of the committee majority, a report may also contain the text of the bill, extensive background information, minority views, and suggested amendments. Some reports, issued by the conference committee made up of members of both houses, resolve differences between versions of a bill passed by the House and the Senate. Only fairly recent committee reports are available free on the Web.

Source: "Committee Reports" on *THOMAS*—http://thomas.loc.gov/
Coverage: 104th Congress (1995/96) to present
Information: The full text of all committee reports printed by the GPO. Reports are provided in text and PDF formats.
Access: From *THOMAS* homepage, under "Committee Information: Committee Reports:" select the Congress you wish to search. Then search by word/phrase, report number, bill number, or committee.
Help: From the "Committee Reports" search page, at the top under "Help," select "Searching Committee Reports"—http://thomas.loc.gov/cp104/srch_crpt.html.

Alternative source: "Senate, House, and Executive Reports" on *GPO Access* —http://www.access.gpo.gov/congress/cong005.html—includes selected Congressional reports since the 104th Congress (1995/96) in both text and PDF formats.

Presidential Messages

As noted above, when signing or vetoing a bill, the president often issues a statement, called a presidential message. Also, a presidential message may accompany a bill introduced into Congress with the president's support. On the Web, sources of presidential messages include the White House Web site, Web versions of House and Senate documents, and the *Congressional Record.*

Source: "White House Virtual Library"—http://library.whitehouse.gov/?request=txt
Coverage: Currently, just this administration (1993) to present
Information: The full text of Press briefings, radio addresses, Executive Orders, and all other publicly released White House publications since the beginning of the Clinton administration.
Access: Select "Archive of All White House Documents." Then search by words or phrases, type of document, and/or date. If you are searching for a statement on a particular bill number, enter only the numerical part of the bill number (e.g. "2646," not "H.R. 2646").

Source: "Senate, House, and Treaty Documents" on *GPO Access*—
http://www.access.gpo.gov/congress/cong006.html
Coverage: 104th (1995–96) to present
Information: The full text of selected House, Senate and Treaty Documents in both text and PDF formats
Access: Enter words or phrases from the full text of the documents. Bill numbers can be searched as phrases. Phrases must be in quotation marks.
Help: "Helpful Hints for Searching Congressional Documents"—
http://www.access.gpo.gov/su_docs/aces/desc011.html
Source: *"Congressional Record* Text on *THOMAS"* (See above.)

Public Laws

As already noted, the GPO first publishes laws in paper as "slip laws." Each public law has its own (chronological) public law number. For example, Public Law 104–32 is the 32nd public law passed in the 104th Congress. These laws are later republished (again, in chronological order) in bound volumes called the *United States Statutes at Large.* A sample citation in the *Statutes* is 92 Stat. 346. This refers to page 346 in the 92nd volume. Every six years the *Statutes* are codified, or arranged by subject, in a new edition of the *United States Code.* The *U.S. Code* includes only the laws that are in effect as of the date of publication, deleting all superseded laws. Consequently, this is the best source for locating the current law on a given subject. A sample citation in the *U.S. Code* is 44 U.S.C. 1913, where 44 is the title number and 1913 is the section number.

Individual laws

Source: "Bill Summary & Status" on *THOMAS*—http://thomas.loc.gov/
Coverage: 101st Congress (1989/90) to present
Information: Full text of public laws in text and PDF formats. Before 1989 only a summary of the legislation is provided.

Access: From the *THOMAS* homepage, under "Bills: Public Laws by Law Number:" select the current Congress, or select "Previous Congresses" and then the Congress you wish to search. Then choose from a list of public law numbers or bill numbers.

Source: "Public Laws" on *GPO Access*—http://www.access.gpo.gov/nara/nara005.html
Coverage: 104th Congress (1995/96) to present
Information: Full text of public laws in both text and PDF formats
Access: Laws can be searched by Congress, public law number, *Statutes at Large* citation, Congressional bill number, or subject.
Help: "Helpful Hints for Searching Public Laws of the 104th Congress."— http://www.access.gpo.gov/su_docs/aces/desc005.html

U.S. Code

Source: "*United States Code*" on *GPO Access*— http://www.access.gpo.gov/congress/cong013.html
Information/coverage: Text of *U.S. Code* as of January 1996
Access: It can be searched by *U.S. Code* citation, public law number, *Statutes* citation, and "section amended by subsequent legislation."
Help: "Helpful Hints for Searching the *United States Code*"— http://www.access.gpo.gov/su_docs/aces/desc007.html

Source: "*United States Code* at Cornell Law School"— http://www.law.cornell.edu:80/uscode/
Information/coverage: Text of *U.S. Code* as of January 1996
Access: Select from a listing of all titles of the *U.S. Code* or from the "Table of Popular Names" of laws. Or search by *U.S. Code* citation or by keyword (searching either the entire *U.S. Code*, or an individual title).

Alternative source: "House Internet Law Library *U.S. Code*"— http://law.house.gov/usc.htm. This web site offers a wide variety of search options.

Finding Information about Legislators

Library patrons often want to know whom their representative or senators are and how to get in touch with them. All members of Congress can now be contacted by e-mail as well as by mail or phone. Sometimes patrons also want to get biographical information about legislators, voting records of legislators, and ratings of legislators by special interest groups.

Directories of Legislators

Source: C-Span's "Find Your Representative"— http://congress.nw.dc.us/c-span/search.html?
Coverage/Information: For current Congress, information on each member includes state, district, party, term, Capitol Hill office address, phone, fax, district office, district

phone, e-mail address, committees, previous occupation, previous political office, home town, education, birthplace and date of birth, spouse, religion, military service, and selected congressional votes. Also includes link to listing of state delegation, office staff, and link to e-mail form for that House member.

Access: Enter zip code, select from an alphabetical listing by name, select a state (for the state delegation), or type in the member's name. A name search can be limited by party, house, or state.

Alternative sources:

There are numerous Congressional directories on the web. Links to many of these are provided on the Library of Congress's "U.S. House Members" web page— http://lcweb.loc.gov/global/legislative/house.html and its "U.S. Senators" page— http://lcweb.loc.gov/global/legislative/senators.html.

Biographies of Legislators

Source: "*Congressional Directory*" on *GPO Access*

Coverage/Information: 104th Congress (1995/96) to present. This source provides information on birth date, home town, education, awards, previous occupations, spouse, children, committees, terms, e-mail address, homepage address, plus office addresses and phone numbers.

Access: To search for a name in the text of the *Congressional Directory*, select a specific directory and enter the name.

Additional help: "Helpful Hints for Searching the *Congressional Directory*"— http://www.access.gpo.gov/su_docs/aces/desc010.html

Alternative sources: Links to Web sites that provide biographies and background information can be found on the Library of Congress's "U.S. House Members" web page—http://lcweb.loc.gov/global/legislative/house.html—and on its "U.S. Senators" page— http://lcweb.loc.gov/global/legislative/senators.html.

Voting Records

Source: *Congressional Quarterly*'s "Vote Watch"— http://pathfinder.com/@@iHj@GDCOJAEAQCLP/CQ/

Information: For each member of the House and Senate, this web site provides information on key votes for the previous eighteen months.

Access: From the "Vote Watch" homepage, select "Latest House Key Vote," "Latest Senate Key Vote," or "Search Past Key Votes." Past key votes for this Congress can be searched by member name. If you don't know the name(s) of your Senators or Representatives, enter your state, district, zip code, popular bill name, keyword or major subject area.

Alternative sources: Lists of links for Web sites which provide voting records for members of the House and Senate can be found on the Library of Congress's Web page "Roll Call Votes and Voting Member Records"— http://lcweb.loc.gov/global/legislative/voting.html.

Ratings of Legislators

Source: *Congressional Quarterly*'s "Rate Your Rep"—
http://voter96.cqalert.com/cq_rate.htm.
Coverage/Information: This Web site tells you how your legislator's positions on ten key issues compare with your own, and also how they compare with the position of other visitors to the Web site.
Access: Type in the last name of a member of the House or Senate, enter a zip code, or select a state and then a legislator. Then fill out a ten-point questionnaire.

Source: "Project Vote Smart"—http://www.vote-smart.org/
Coverage/Information: For members of Congress (and candidates), this Web site reports performance evaluations that have been provided by a wide range of interest groups.
Access: On the "Project Vote Smart" homepage select "Candidates and Elected Officials," then "Congress." Select "click here to find members of Congress by name." Alternatively, you can enter a zip code to find the name of your legislator. Or you can select a state, then select Senate or a Congressional district.

Alternative sources: Library of Congress's "Roll Call Votes and Member Voting Records"—http://lcweb.loc.gov/global/legislative/voting.html—provides links to a number of Web sites concerned with ratings of legislators by special interest groups.

Web Guides and Additional Resources

This lesson covers only some of the legislative information on the World Wide Web. Additional Web sites that are especially useful are listed below.

Explanations of the legislative process
"How Our Laws Are Made," by Charles W. Johnson, House Parliamentarian—
http://thomas.loc.gov/home/lawsmade.toc.html. The emphasis of this document is upon legislative procedure in the House.

"Enactment of a Law, " by Robert V. Dove, Senate Parliamentarian—
http://thomas.loc.gov/home/enactment/enactlawtoc.html. This emphasis of this document is upon legislative procedure in the Senate.

Guides for Searching *GPO Access* and *THOMAS*
"GPO Access Searching Tips," Georgetown University Law Library
http://www.ll.georgetown.edu/wtaylor/gposrch.html

"Guide to Searching *GPO Access*," Larry Schankman, Mansfield (PA) University
http://www.clark.net/pub/lschank/web/gpo.html

"Library Guide Series: Legislative Research with *THOMAS*," Larry Schankman, Mansfield (PA) University
http://www.clark.net/pub/lschank/web/mythomas.html

General guides

Legislative Information, Larry Schankman, Mansfield (PA) University
http://www.clark.net/pub/lschank/web/bills.html
This Web site includes guides to *GPO Access*, House of Representatives Web sites, Library of Congress's Federal Legislation Database (LOCIS), Senate Home Page, *THOMAS*, locating members of Congress and their voting records, and additional information sources.

"Legislative Histories," Grace York, University of Michigan Documents Center.
http://www.lib.umich.edu/libhome/Documents.center/legishis.html
This source provides tips on researching legislative history and links to important legislative web sites.

Lists of More Legislative Web Sites

Library of Congress's "U.S. Legislative Branch"
http://lcweb.loc.gov/global/legislative/congress.html

Library of Congress's listing of "Congressional Mega Sites"
http://lcweb.loc.gov/global/legislative/mega.html

Hands-on Exercises

The research questions that follow are simply a listing. Detailed instructions for the trainees will be included only on the accompanying disk. The reason is for the convenience of the librarians who use these exercises; they can easily be customized from the disk version. Two examples are included in the chapter as they will appear on the disk.

- Find a history of S.1970 from the 104th Congress. What was the short title of the bill? What was it designed to do? Did it become a law?

- How many senators voted for, and how many voted against S.2307 on July 24, 1998?

- Find the full text of a bill entitled the "Antiterrorism and Effective Death Penalty Act of 1996."

- Find a July 1998 statement made by Rep. Knollenberg on the floor of the House concerning the Kyoto Treaty.

- Find the text of a hearing on "U.S. Counter-Narcotics Policy Towards Colombia" held at the end of March 1998.

- Find President Clinton's Oct. 10, 1997 letter to the House explaining his reasons for vetoing H.R. 1122 (which would have outlawed "partial birth" abortions.)

- Try to locate the text of the "Middle East Peace Facilitation Act of 1993" (P.L.103-125).

- Find the section of the *U.S. Code* which authorizes the "restraint, regulation, and removal" of aliens who are citizens of a hostile country in time of war. (It is in Title 50 which deals with "War and National Defense.")

- Find the name and e-mail address of your representative using just your zip code. Also find a biography of your legislator.

- Using *Congressional Quarterly*'s "Rate Your Rep" Web site, find out how closely your representative's positions correspond to your own.

- How does the AFL-CIO rate your representative?

- Find the voting record of one of your senators for the previous eighteen months.

Legislative Research Exercise

Find a history of S.1970 from the 104th Congress. What was the short title of the bill? What was it designed to do? Did it become a law?

Step 1   What sources did you use to find this information? List them.

Step 2   Document your search strategy.

Legislative Research Exercise

How many senators voted for, and how many voted against S.2307 on July 24, 1998?

Step 1   What sources did you use to find this information? List them.

Step 2   Document your search strategy.

Notes:

Shakespeare Resources

Katherine Furlong

User Education and Electronic Resources Librarian
University of Maine at Farmington

Introduction

Shakespeare questions:

- Do you know your folios from your quartos?
- Where is the Forest of Arden?
- Can you summarize *Cymbeline*?
- Is it all Greek to you?

While the breadth of Shakespeare scholarship is unparalleled, you can gain an understanding of basic reference resources without a Ph.D. in English Literature. This training session will give a broad overview of resources available, specialized Shakespeare vocabulary, how to approach Shakespeare topics, and some ideas on tackling tricky Bardic reference questions.

There are many types of Shakespeare reference tools, and the variety can be overwhelming to those just starting to work on the reference desk. This session is by no means exhaustive, but it does cover the basics.

Goals and Objectives of the Instruction and Training

While you will need to set your own goals to suit the needs of your students, the goal used in developing this session was to familiarize new reference workers with standard Shakespeare reference resources.

The hands-on exercises included at the end of the lesson will allow the participants to immediately apply their new knowledge using real-life reference questions. You may wish to develop an evaluation form to gauge your effectiveness as an instructor and your students' comprehension.

Components of the Instruction and Training

Preparing Yourself

Just as Shakespeare's plays are best understood through performance, reference resources are best learned through use. There are many more resources listed in this chapter than can realistically be covered in one session. The key is to choose and discuss those available and frequently used in your library. Remember that the hands-on exercises should make students use the resources available, so choose questions that may be answered by resources you have on hand! The exercises may be used by groups, or by students working individually. I prefer to talk about and demonstrate resources in context, going to the reference stacks to discuss reference books, and the index shelves to discuss indexes. This may not be possible in your library.

You may wish to reproduce the research basics handout included on the disk. Don't forget that this information may be overwhelming, so brush up your *own* Shakespeare before starting to teach!

Background & Research Challenges

The volume of research on Shakespeare in a given year is staggering; the 1996 *MLA International Bibliography* has 751 Shakespeare entries. To an undergraduate facing a research project, these numbers are daunting. To a librarian trying to help, it can prove either fascinating or fantastically frustrating. This volume of research makes the need for reference tools even greater: directories, bibliographies and research guides can be valuable tools. The key is to get researchers (and the librarians helping them) to make use of these tools. Some background and basic concepts can help.

Vocabulary

There are some specific terms that researchers and librarians should be familiar with when using Shakespearean scholarship. While entire dictionaries of Shakespeare words and terms exist (see *Dictionaries and Encyclopedias*), a few key terms are included here, and on the research basics handout included on the disk.

Concordance	This is an alphabetical index of the words used in a work or collected works of an author. If you have a burning desire to know how often Shakespeare used the word "loon," or which play contains the phrase "cream-faced loon," a concordance may come in handy.
Edition	The important thing to remember is that all texts of Shakespeare are editions; since none of the author's own play manuscripts survived, there is no definitive "author's cut." Most modern readers use what are called editorial reconstructions; some may ask to see facsimiles of Folios and Quartos (see below).
Folio	A folio is made by folding over a printer's sheet once to create two leaves (four pages); most commonly used to describe the editions of Shakespeare's work published after his death. There were four 17th century folios; the First Folio (F1) was printed in 1623. The other Folios are commonly abbreviated F2 (1632), F3 (1663) and F4 (1685).
Quarto	Another term used to designate printing size; the printer's sheet is folded twice to create four leaves (eight pages). About 20 Shakespeare plays were published in quarto size before the publication of the First Folio.

Variorum   This is an edition of a book, or work, with the text and notes of previous editors and commentators. Notes of textual changes are included. They are useful because there is no definitive edition of Shakespeare's work.

You may also want to remind your trainees that, as with any discipline, there are conventions for abbreviating and citing Shakespeare's work. There are standard abbreviations for the play titles, (most works that use them provide a key), and for finding specific points in the text. Generally the play's name will be followed by the act, scene, and line numbers. Therefore, a reference to HAM 1.01.44 would mean *Hamlet*, Act I, Scene One, line 44 *"it harrows me with fear and wonder."*

Shakespeare in the Library

LC classification

Browsing the shelves for Shakespeare resources is made easier if you are aware that the LC classification scheme has subdivisions worked out within the schedules for Shakespeare. Each play has its own class number: single editions of *All's Well That Ends Well* may be found at PR 2801; *Antony and Cleopatra* at PR 2802, *As You Like It* at PR 2803 and so forth alphabetically through all the play titles. Criticism about specific plays is classed with the play; general criticism is classed separately.

The base class number for Shakespeare in the Dewey Decimal classification is 822.33. Libraries using the Dewey system have the option to subarrange works so that all general works, plays and criticism of plays are shelved together. Check with your cataloging department or browse your shelves to see what students confront when looking for Shakespeare materials in your library.

Searching the catalog

You may wish to point out that author or subject searches in your library catalog for "Shakespeare, William" are probably overwhelming. The more specific you can be, the better. *The Library of Congress Subject Headings* uses Shakespeare as the example of subdivisions usable under any literary author heading; you will find many pages showing the right format to use for those subjects. One of the most useful subdivisions is "—Criticism and interpretation" for narrowing searches from editions of works to criticism of works. Be sure to discuss the subject headings used in your library with the trainees.

Keyword searches in an online catalog for "Shakespeare and Hamlet" or "Hamlet and criticism," for example, are simpler and can be very successful. You may also perform keyword searches for reference resources, such as "Shakespeare and dictionary" or "Shakespeare and quotations."

Selected Reference Resources for Shakespeare

Those sources that are available in electronic format (CD-ROM, internet subscription) will be marked with a triple asterisk ***. In this chapter, the resources are arranged as follows:

Shakespeare's Life (biographies)

General questions about Shakespeare's life and times may be concisely answered with any encyclopedia. Most Shakespeare guides and handbooks also include a brief biographical sketch. You can locate biographies of Shakespeare by searching your library catalog for the topic:

Shakespeare, William, 1564–1616—Biography

Shakespeare's Theater

Many researchers seek to understand Shakespeare's dramas by taking into account the theaters for which they were written. Requests for pictures of the Globe Theater are common; the recent reconstruction of the Globe in London has also sparked interest in the stage where many plays were originally performed. Again, pictures of the Globe and other Renaissance theaters are included in most any encyclopedia or Shakespeare handbook; books on the plays in performance may be located by searching the terms:

Shakespeare, William, 1564–1616—Stage history—To 1625
Theater—England—History (may add 16th century, 17th century, etc.)

International Shakespeare Globe Centre
http://www.shakespeares-globe.org/
This is the official web site of the *International Shakespeare Globe Centre*. It links to information on the reconstruction of the Globe, with a virtual tour of the theater and information on the plays in performance.

Shakespeare's Sources

Ever wonder where Shakespeare learned his Roman history? If *Romeo and Juliet* was an original story? While many Shakespeare handbooks and editions have notes on sources, the standard and most comprehensive resource is Geoffrey Bullough's 8-volume set, *Narrative and Dramatic Sources of Shakespeare*, 1957–1975.

General Guides and Handbooks

The Cambridge Companion to Shakespeare Studies. 1986.
Stanley Wells has edited a series of essays covering the most common areas of Shakespeare research.

Outlines of Shakespeare's Plays. 1935.
The authors provide an act-by-act synopsis of each play, with brief essays on Shakespeare's life, theater, and sources. Suggestions for reading are understandably dated.

Shakespeare: A Study and Research Guide. 1995 ed.
The heart of this title is "A guide to the resources," but authors, Bergeron and DeSousa, have included a chapter on preparing a research paper on a Shakespearean topic.

Shakespeare for Students. 1992.
A concise source for beginning students of Shakespeare, offering plot summaries, critical reviews and sources for further study for nine of the most often taught plays. This work is edited by Mark W. Scott.

Dictionaries and Encyclopedias

A Dictionary of Who, What and Where in Shakespeare: a comprehensive guide to Shakespeare's plays, characters and contemporaries. 1997.
1,000 entries cover the plays and characters, with supplemental information on Shakespeare's life and the Elizabethan Theater. The title has the Royal Shakespeare Company seal of approval.

The Reader's Encyclopedia of Shakespeare. 1966.
More than 2,700 entries on all aspects of Shakespeare: plays, poems, life, performances, actors and scholarship are included. It is comprehensive in scope.

Shakespeare A to Z: the essential reference to his plays, his poems, his life, his times and more. 1990.
A self-declared "non-scholarly" work, it includes entries for characters, summaries of plays, information on major actors, scholars, and Shakespearean lore. A very useful tool for students. It is a Facts on File Publication by Charles Boyce.

A Shakespeare Glossary. 1986 ed.
This is a concise source for definitions of words in the Shakespearean canon. It is a useful resource for obscure or obsolete words; it also covers proper nouns and technical terms.

Shakespeare-Lexicon: A Complete Dictionary of the English Words, Phrases and Constructions in the Works of the Poet. 1968 ed., rev. and enl.
As the title suggests, this two-volume set covers all of the words in Shakespeare; not limited to obscure or obsolete terms.

Other General Reference Resources

Other useful general reference books include: *The Oxford Companion to English Literature*, (rev. ed., 1995); Cuddon, John A. *A Dictionary of Literary Terms and Terminology* (3rd ed., 1991); Abrams, M.H. *A Glossary of Literary Terms* (6th ed., 1993); and *Brewer's Dictionary of Phrase and Fable* (14th ed., 1989). Most general encyclopedias include synopses of Shakespeare's plays and sonnets with varying degrees of criticism and interpretation. And don't forget the *Oxford English Dictionary* (2nd ed., 1989–)! ***

Bibliographies and Indexes

The Essential Shakespeare: An Annotated Bibliography of Major Modern Studies. 1993. Larry S. Champion has included about 1,800 annotated entries covering "the most important criticism on Shakespeare in the twentieth century."—*Pref.* Comprehensive author, title and subject indexes are included.

Shakespeare Index: An Annotated Bibliography of Critical Articles on the Plays 1959–1983. 1992.
This is a useful tool for finding articles on specific aspects of the plays; multiple indices are included. While not a basic tool; it is useful for more advanced students and researchers.

World Shakespeare Bibliography ***
Issued as part of, and often shelved with, the *Shakespeare Quarterly*; this bibliography covers books, articles, book reviews, dissertations and productions of Shakespeare's plays. It is an essential reference resource. It is also available on CD-ROM which continues in part the annual issue of *Shakespeare Quarterly* entitled "World Shakespeare Bibliography." When this database is complete, it will provide annotated entries for all important books, articles, book reviews, dissertations, theatrical productions, reviews of productions, audiovisual materials, electronic media, and other scholarly and popular materials related to Shakespeare, and published or produced since 1900.

General indexes are also useful if specific bibliographies are not available in your library. The most useful literary index for Shakespeare resources remains:

MLA: An International Bibliography of Books and Articles on the Modern Languages and Literatures, 1969— ***
MLA is the standard index for scholarly literary research. It is available in print and electronic format.

Other standard print and electronic indexes that cover Shakespeare include *Periodical Abstracts ***, Expanded Academic ASAP ***, Readers' Guide to Periodical Literature ***, Humanities Index ***and Essay and General Literature Index.* General periodical and newspaper indexes are especially useful for coverage of performances such as movie and play reviews appearing in *The New York Times ***.

Editions

As noted before, all texts of Shakespeare are editions; since none of the author's own play manuscripts survived, there is no definitive "author's cut." Most modern readers use editorial reconstructions. There are many quality editions in print today. Notable single editions of plays include the Cambridge University Press, Oxford University Press, and New Folger Shakespeare Library series. Many libraries include an edition of the complete works in their reference collection. The *Riverside Shakespeare* (2nd ed. 1997) remains a reliable standard and is the basis of the *Harvard Concordance*. An Internet resource for editons and adaptations follows.

Literature Online
http://lion.chadwyck.com/
This Internet resource is from Chadwyck-Healey. Subscribers may use a variety of literary databases and reference works, including a special section on Editions and Adaptations of Shakespeare (1511–1911).

Concordances

The Harvard Concordance to Shakespeare. 1973.
This title is a complete, one-volume concordance to every word in the plays and poems of Shakespeare. It uses the modern day spelling of the *Riverside Shakespeare*.

Oxford Shakespeare Concordances. 1969–1972.
A separate volume is available for each of Shakespeare's plays.

Quotations

Bartlett's Familiar Shakespearean Quotations
http://the-tech.mit.edu/Shakespeare/Quotes/bartlett.html
This site is online from Jeremy Hylton at MIT. If specific Shakespeare quotation books are not available, general quotation books, such as Bartlett's *Familiar Quotations* *** or the *Columbia Dictionary of Quotations* have good coverage of Shakespeare.

The Home Book of Shakespeare Quotations. 1937.
The subtitle reads "being also a concordance and a glossary of the unique words & phrases in the plays & poems." It was arranged and edited by Burton Egbert Stevenson.

The Quotable Shakespeare. 1988.
This work includes thorough indexing of about 6,500 quotations from Shakespeare.

Characters

Longman Guide to Shakespeare's Characters: A Who's Who of Shakespeare. 1985.

Shakespeare's Characters for Students. 1997.
Each play is given a chapter, with plot summaries, "modern connections" and an alphabetical listing of the characters. A character/topic index provides easy access and cross-references.

The Shakespeare Name Dictionary. 1995.
D.J. Madison has provided an alphabetical listing of "every name, proper adjective, official title, literary and musical title and place name that appears in the text of the complete plays and poems of William Shakespeare."—*Introd.*

Shakespeare in Performance—Reviews of plays

The *World Shakespeare Bibliography* and any index that covers *The New York Times* are important resources for reviews of live Shakespeare performances. See also the chapter on reviews in volume 1, p. 150–163.

Shakespeare in Performance—Costuming and Staging

Shakespeare: An Illustrated Stage History. 1996.
Most single play editions, such as *The Oxford Shakespeare*, contain pictures of performances; general theatrical costume books, however, are also useful. Keyword searches in your library catalog for "Shakespeare and dramatic production" or "Shakespeare and stage history" may produce relevant books.

Shakespeare on Film

Shakespeare on Screen: An International Filmography and Videography. 1990.
Rothwell and Milzer have provided a collected body of Shakespeare available on film and video from 1889 to 1989.

The Internet Movie Database
http://www.imdb.com/
This is an excellent resource for movies, cast lists and reviews.

Shakespeare on the Internet

The *Complete Works of William Shakespeare* is available on several Internet servers; one of the most reliable is MIT's—http://the-tech.mit.edu/Shakespeare/works.html.

Mr. William Shakespeare and the Internet
http://daphne.palomar.edu/shakespeare/
This site includes a Shakespeare time line, genealogical chart, bibliography, and annotated links to other scholarly and frivolous Shakespeare sites. It also includes HTML

versions of Charles and Mary Lamb's *Tales from Shakespeare*, the prefatory materials from the First Folio and the introduction to Nicholas Rowe's 1709 edition of Shakespeare's plays.

Surfing with the Bard
http://www.ulen.com/shakespeare/
This is Amy Ulen's site with resources for teachers and students; especially notable for *The Undiscover'd Country*; information on *Star Trek* and Shakespeare. It is the Internet, after all!

Hands-on Exercises

The exercises below are set up on the disk with detailed instructions for participants; two examples have been set up as worksheets in the chapter. Each participant will have a set of 3–4 Shakespeare questions to answer. For your convenience, you may print each set as a separate page for easy distribution, and/or customize them to fit the needs of your situation. Each worksheet is constructed to require the participants to make hands-on use of a Shakespeare concordance, another Shakespeare reference work (generally a Shakespeare encyclopedia or the *Oxford Companion to English Literature*), and a bibliography or database. Participants should be encouraged to use the *World Shakespeare Bibliography* if available, however, the questions are answerable with a good general periodical index such as *The Readers' Guide to Periodical Literature* *** or *Expanded Academic ASAP* ***.

1. Use a Shakespeare concordance to identify the source of the following quotation: "The plague of Greece upon thee, thou mongrel beef-witted lord!"
2. Use a Shakespeare encyclopedia and the *Oxford Companion to English Literature* to determine the sources of Shakespeare's *Troilus and Cressida*. Which resources had the most complete information? Did they agree?
3. Paris is the son of Hecuba and the King of Troy in *Troilus and Cressida*. Does Shakespeare use this name in any other plays?

1. Use a Shakespeare concordance to identify the source of the following quotation "If music be the food of love, play on."
2. Using the *World Shakespeare Bibliography* or a general periodical index, find a review of the Broadway production of the musical *Play On!* by Sheldon Epps and Cheryl L. West. (First staged in 1996.) Why would a review of this work be in a Shakespeare index?
3. Use a Shakespeare encyclopedia to determine the purpose of instrumental music in productions of Shakespeare's time. Where did the musicians perform?

1. Use a Shakespeare concordance to determine which play begins with the following line: "O for a muse of fire..."
2. A committed literature student is looking for the name of the muse of fire. Use a literary encyclopedia or dictionary to find the names of the muses. Is there a muse of fire? Is there a literary convention about invoking muses?
3. *Henry V* was one of the four plays produced in the opening season of the New Globe Theatre in 1997. Who directed it? Can you find a review of the production?

1. Use a Shakespeare concordance to determine the source of the following quotation: "Nature teaches beasts to know their friends."
2. A faculty member has a partial citation for an article written by J. Plotz on a Shakespeare tragedy. She suspects that the article was written in the mid-1990s. Use the *World Shakespeare Bibliography* or a general periodical index to find the full citation. Can you find a summary of the article?
3. Francis Bacon, Christopher Marlowe, Edward de Vere, 17th Earl of Oxford and Roger Manners, 5th Earl of Rutland all have something in common: they are all *claimants*. What does this mean? Use a Shakespeare encyclopedia or handbook to find out!

1. Use a Shakespeare concordance to identify the source of the following quotation: "He capers nimbly in a lady's chamber to the lascivious pleasings of a lute."
2. An eager student wants to prove that Shakespeare wrote the play, *A Yorkshire Tragedy*. Use a Shakespeare encyclopedia and *The Oxford Companion to English Literature* to find information on the play. Which folios included the play? Upon what event was the play based? Who wrote the play? Which resources had the most complete information? Did they agree?
3. In how many film versions of Shakespeare has Kenneth Branagh appeared? How many has he directed? Use the *Internet Movie Database* http://www.imdb.com or another film bibliography to find the answer. If you used the *Internet Movie Database*, how current was the information? How reliable?

1. Use a Shakespeare concordance to identify the source of the following phrase: "making the beast with two backs."
2. Use the *World Shakespeare Bibliography* to find a review of the 1995 film version of *Othello*. Then look for a review using a general periodical index, and the Internet Movie Database http://www.imdb.com. Did you find the same reviews? Is there a difference between the three resources?
3. Use a Shakespeare handbook or encyclopedia to find the names of the members of the Lord Chamberlain's Men. When was the company's first performance?

1. Use a Shakespeare concordance to determine the source of the following quotation: "I see a voice!"
2. Peter Brook directed a groundbreaking production of *A Midsummer Night's Dream* in 1970, which toured in the United States during the following year. Find a review of the production using the *New York Times Index*.
3. Using the *World Shakespeare Bibliography, The Essential Shakespeare: An Annotated Bibliography* or a general periodical index, find subsequent criticism of the Brook production.
4. The Brook production has been called "post-modern." Use a literary dictionary or glossary to define modernism and postmodernism.

1. Use a Shakespeare concordance to determine the source of Aldous Huxley's book title, *Brave New World*. What is the complete quotation?
2. A student is looking for information on the relationship between Shakespeare's *The Tempest* and the Beethoven Piano Sonata No. 17 in D Minor "Tempest" (opus 31, no.2). Using the *World Shakespeare Bibliography* and other indexes, locate an article linking the two works.
3. How many First Folios does the Folger Shakespeare Library hold? How does a scholar gain access to the Folger Library Reading Room? Use a Shakespeare encyclopedia or handbook to find the answers, then look for the same information on the Folger's web site http://www.folger.edu/. Do the sources agree?

Exercise—Shakespeare Resources

Using the reference tools discussed in class, try to answer the three reference questions listed below. You may need to consult more than one resource for each question.

No. 1   Use a Shakespeare concordance to identify the source of the following quotation:

        "The plague of Greece upon thee, thou mongrel beef-witted lord!"

        Concordance consulted:

        Play:

        Act:

        Scene:

        Line:

No. 2   Use a Shakespeare encyclopedia and the *Oxford Companion to English Literature* to determine the sources of Shakespeare's *Troilus and Cressida*:

        Reference works consulted:

        Answer(s):

Which resources had the most complete information?

Did they agree?

No. 3   Paris is the son of Hecuba and the King of Troy in *Troilus and Cressida*. Does Shakespeare use this name in any other plays?

Reference works consulted:

Answer(s):

Exercise—Shakespeare Resources

Using the reference tools discussed in class, try to answer the three reference questions listed below. You may need to consult more than one resource for each question.

No. 1   Use a Shakespeare concordance to identify the source of the following quotation:

"He capers nimbly in a lady's chamber to the lascivious pleasings of a lute"

Concordance consulted:

Play:

Act:

Scene:

Line:

No. 2   An eager student wants to prove that Shakespeare wrote the play, *A Yorkshire Tragedy*. Use a Shakespeare encyclopedia and *The Oxford Companion to English Literature* to find information on the play. Which folios included the play? Upon what event was the play based? Who wrote the play?

Resources used:

Answers:

Which resources had the most complete information? Did they agree?

No. 3   In how many film versions of Shakespeare has Kenneth Branagh appeared?
How many has he directed? Use the *Internet Movie Database*
http://www.imdb.com or another film bibliography to find the answer.

Bibliography/database used:

Answer:

If you used the *Internet Movie Database*, how current was the information?
How reliable?

Shakespeare Research Basics

Some specific terms that researchers and librarians should be familiar with when using Shakespeare scholarship:

Concordance   This is an alphabetical index of the words used in a work or collected works of an author. If you have a burning desire to know how often Shakespeare used the word "loon," or which play contains the phrase "cream-faced loon," a concordance may come in handy.

Edition   The important thing to remember is that all texts of Shakespeare are editions; since none of the author's own play manuscripts survived, there is no definitive "author's cut." Most modern readers use what are called editorial reconstructions; some may ask to see facsimiles of Folios and Quartos (see below).

Folio   A folio is made by folding over a printer's sheet once to create two leaves (four pages); most commonly used to describe the editions of Shakespeare's work published after his death. There were four 17th century folios; the First Folio (F1) was printed in 1623. The other Folios are commonly abbreviated F2 (1632), F3 (1663) and F4 (1685).

Quarto   Another term used to designate printing size; the printer's sheet is folded twice to create four leaves (eight pages). About 20 Shakespeare plays were published in quarto size before the publication of the First Folio.

Variorum   This is an edition of a book, or work, with the text and notes of previous editors and commentators. Notes of textual changes are included. They are useful because there is no definitive edition of Shakespeare's work.

Shakespeare in the Library

LC classification: Browsing the shelves for Shakespeare resources is made easier if you are aware that the LC classification scheme has subdivisions worked out within the schedules for Shakespeare. Each play has its own class number: single editions of *All's Well That Ends Well* may be found at PR 2801; *Antony and Cleopatra* at PR 2802, *As You Like It* at PR 2803 and so forth alphabetically through all the play titles. Criticism about specific plays is classed with the play; general criticism is classed separately.

Searching the catalog: Author or subject searches in your library catalog for "Shakespeare, William" are probably overwhelming. The more specific you can be, the better. Keyword searches for "Shakespeare and Hamlet" or "Hamlet and criticism" are usually much more successful. You may also perform keyword searches for reference resources, such as "Shakespeare and dictionary" or "Shakespeare and quotations."

Sports and Leisure

MARY ELLEN COLLINS, PH.D.

Education/Health, Kinesiology & Leisure Studies Bibliographer
PURDUE UNIVERSITY LIBRARIES

Introduction

Sport and leisure literature covers a wide gamut in the reference field, an indication of the range of interest that people have about this discipline. Personalities in sports dominate the field of interest, as the media focuses on figures that capture the headlines. A segment of this literature includes games, some of which may border on sports activities.

Of course, records of achievements in every sport, especially the college and professional teams, and the Olympic competition, invite universal interest, and may be found in several locations, as are biographical sketches. Beyond these two categories, there are handbooks for those who want to know how to play a game or perform a sport, dictionaries for the new terms that come into use, directories for those looking for good camps for their children.

A growing category of interest is that of the sociology and psychology of sports, especially for women and children. The literature in this group discusses the ways in which women have changed sports and views on women's physiology. Drug use in sports occupies another large section of this category. Fitness and appropriate clothing, especially shoes, are concerns of every participant in a sport, and the literature is replete with information on these topics.

Perhaps the most salient characteristic of this literature is the fact that information can be found in more than one place. This is especially true for biographical information. In some cases a person's biographical sketch will include only sport performance data, but not personal information.

Periodical literature in these fields, like any other, is subject to multiple title changes. Where possible, the date the periodical began is shown. In some cases, title changes have been substantial enough that the date only reflects the beginning of the latest title/version of the periodical.

The literature presented here represents a typical collection that might be found in a small to medium-sized library. The purpose of this collection is to cover as wide a spectrum of the information available on sports and games as might be feasible within the scope and budget of such an institution. It is hopeful that most questions can be answered on site with this group of reference books. Detailed information on specific sports would be contingent on the culture of the area in which the library is located.

Components of the Instruction and Training

Objectives

- To understand the variety and types of sport and leisure information.
- To use finding aids in reference books, such as indexes, tables of contents and inherent arrangement (such as alphabetical) to locate information effectively.
- To use keyword searching effectively in electronic catalogs to hone in on exact subjects. Keywords can get one into the general subject territory; subject headings can lead to the specific location of record(s).

Library of Congress subject headings are most commonly used in the large libraries. Some examples are:

> Olympics—History
> Football—United States—Statistics
> Basketball—Records
> Leisure—Bibliography
> Sports—Rules
> Camps—United States—Directories
> Sports—Dictionaries
> Athletes—United States—Biography—Dictionaries

Some examples of Sears subject headings are:

> Camping
> Olympic games
> Special Olympics
> Drugs and sports
> Sports facilities
> Sports—Corrupt practices

- To use periodical indexes to find articles in magazines.
- To understand how to use both an electronic periodical index as well as a print periodical index.
- To know how to find information in more than one place.

As part of the instruction process, the trainees might be invited to suggest the best possible resources for some of the questions, such as:

> When was Tiger Woods born?
> When was the Borg-Warner Trophy first awarded, and to whom?
> Describe "hypoxia." Whom does it affect?
> Where did the phrase "on deck" come from, and what does it mean?

Selected Reference Resources for Sports and Leisure

Those sources that are available in electronic format (CD-ROM, internet subscription) will be marked with a triple asterisk ***. In this chapter, the resources are arranged as follows:
    Almanacs and Yearbooks
    Bibliographies
    Biography
    Chronologies and Histories
    Dictionaries and Encyclopedias
    Guides and Handbooks
    Indexes and Abstracts

Almanacs and Yearbooks

The...ESPN Information Please Sports Almanac, 1990–
This almanac is divided by sports, and by some key events. There is also a section on sports personalities.

Guinness Book of Records, 1990–
This collection of record achievements is classified by broad subject category, with one category for sports and an index. The former title was *Guinness Book of World Records*, 1955–1989.

Bibliographies

Many hundreds of bibliographies have been compiled that deal with sports in general and on the individual sports. The titles listed below are a sample of what is available.

An Annotated Bibliography of Latin American Sport; Pre-Conquest to the Present. 1989.
Sports in Latin America have traditionally been very important and the compiler has included sources on and examples of sport in fiction, poetry, and other literary and artistic genre because he found them invaluable reflections of the Latin American Sports world.—*Pref.*

Social Issues in Contemporary Sport: A Resource Guide. 1994.
This is a bibliography of books and articles in the field of sports. It includes chapters on doping and legal issues, among many others. It provides a useful guide to subject coverage of sports topics.

Sports Ethics in America: A Bibliography, 1970–1990. 1992.
This bibliography was compiled because sports ethics is both a significant and hot topic in American society. It includes books and articles from scholars and also works from journalists, current and ex-athletes, ex-coaches, and other writers who have addressed the social and ethical issues of sports in contemporary society.—*Introd.*

Biography Sources

Biographical Dictionary of American Sports.
Separate volumes have been published for football, baseball, basketball; and other sports; supplements are issued as single volumes. Both men and women covered. The index entries include people, sports, places, and events.

Current Biography, 1940– (annual cumulations)
Each issue provides biographical essays on current personalities in politics, entertainment, sports, broadcasting, business, etc. The index is cumulated every decade.

Encyclopedia of Women and Sports. 1996.
Largely biographical entries are covered in this title, but it also includes entries for the sports themselves, the associations, and events. Some personal information for sports figures that is not always found in other sports biographical sources is included.

Outstanding Women Athletes: Who They Are, and How They Influenced Sports in America. 1992.
The emphasis of this title is the history of women's sports, specifically of women in the Olympics and in American sports. Biographies of American women in sports in the past as well as in the present are included. Indexes are by sport of the athletes and by names of athletes themselves.

Chronologies and Histories

The Baseball Encyclopedia: *The Complete and Official Record of Major League Baseball*. 1996 ed.
A brief history of baseball, outstanding achievements, leaders in batting, pitching and fielding are listed, showing their scores for a single season, and for a lifetime. Teams and players are given, and many statistics. Charts are plentiful.

Encyclopedia of World Sport from Ancient Times to the Present. 1996.
This arrangement is alphabetical of over 250 individual sports and sport topics that reflect the historical and international development of sport from ancient times to the present. This is evident in the kind of sports that have been admitted to the Olympic Games. The set is paged continuously and has a thorough index.

The Football Encyclopedia: The Complete History of Professional Football from 1892 to the Present. 1994 ed.
This encyclopedia chronicles the beginnings of pro football, and the development of the National Football League, the National Football Conference, and the American Football Conference. Discussion centers on the way the game has been played, including charts of positions, scores and players throughout history.

The Official NBA Basketball Encyclopedia. 1994 ed.
Included are the histories of the National Basketball Association and the American Basketball Association, outstanding highlights, records, Hall of Fame nominees, official rules, among other topics. The index is inclusive of sports figures, games, and events.

Dictionaries and Encyclopedias

Coaches' Guide to Drugs and Sport. 1996.
This is a handbook for use by coaches who deal with the issue of drugs and doping in sporting activities. It is arranged topically, with an excellent appendix to various drugs such as smokeless tobacco among others. It contains information on what the drug is, how it is used, its short-term effects, long-term effects and connection with athletics.

Encyclopedia of Sports Science. 1997.
Volume 1 discusses the specific sports and families of sports, including the skills needed in the development of the sport, and other related topics. The second volume deals with the human physiology—aging, the female body, nutrition, rehabilitation, and other topics frequently connected with sport. Statistics are frequently included.

Ergogenic Aids in Sport. 1983.
The chapters deal with drugs with a positive and negative effect in sport. One chapter deals with anabolic steroids, and has a section showing especially the detrimental physical effects on women. There is an extensive bibliography.

Guide to ACA-Accredited Camps, 1982–
This guide lists approximately 2,000 camps in the United States which are accredited by the ACA because they meet its standards of safety, health and program quality. They are indexed by location, activity, and special needs.

The Official Encyclopedia of Bridge. 1995 ed.
This source is considered the authoritative reference on contract bridge. It presents the history, detailed playing of the game, and terminology.

Guides and Handbooks

Opportunities in Sports & Athletics Careers. 1999 ed.
This source deals with a wider variety of career possibilities in sports, including those in sports medicine, fitness (such as athletic trainer), professional athletics and business.

Complete Book of Games and Stunts. 1956.
This, while an older title, does contain many games that can be used for various occasions, including traveling. A good source to keep everyone entertained.

The Complete Book of the Winter Olympics. 1998 ed.
The Complete Book of the Summer Olympics. 1996 ed.
These two sources are basic guides to the Olympic Games, giving history, winners, and sports in separate sections.

NCAA Basketball: The Official...Men's College Basketball Records Book, 1915–
Records for all divisions and individuals, winners of awards, championships, playing
rules, etc. are included.

NCAA Championships: Official National Collegiate Championships Record Book, 1978–
This source, too, is an annual collection of records, specifically for college sports.

*The New Complete Hoyle: The Authoritative Guide to the Official Rules of All Popular
Games of Skill and Chance.* 1991 ed.
This title, alphabetically arranged by game, includes all kinds of card games and other
games such as Backgammon, Bingo, Checkers, Dominoes, etc.

101 Dance Games for Children: Fun and Creativity with Movement. 1996.
This title covers dance activities for young children aged four years through adults.

Opportunities in Nonprofit Organization Careers. 1994.
This source covers all types of nonprofit organizations as they might present work
opportunities. Short essays on hobbies and on sports issue caveats for job hopefuls, and
include a list of associations that one may check out.

The Oxford Guide to Card Games. 1990.
This reference presents the context of card games historically and socially. It does cover
some rules. Indexes are included.

Parlor Cards. 1999.
This titles covers card games as well as hobbies and games, magic and puzzles.

Sports and the Law: Major Legal Cases. 1996.
The essays cover major cases and court decisions in sports cases, including those dealing
with equality. Helpful indexes are included.

Sports Rules Encyclopedia. 1990 ed.
This is a comprehensive source for rules for a wide variety of individual sports, such as
archery, badminton, golf, bowling, soccer, and volleyball, among many others. This
source is useful for anyone directing organized sports programs.

Sports Talk: A Dictionary of Sports Metaphors. 1989.
A dictionary of phrases used in our everyday language that have come from sports is the
focus of this title.

Water Fun: Swimming Instruction and Water Games for the Whole Family. 1990.
Many excellent black and white photographs, along with diagrams and drawings, enhance
this thorough treatment of swimming activities. It includes the basic strokes of
swimming, exercising, games, safety, and first aid. It is indexed.

Indexes and Abstracts—Print and Electronic

The field of sports is covered in many general and specialized indexes and abstracts.

ERIC ***

Ethnic Newswatch ***

MEDLINE ***

National Newspaper Index ***

Periodical Abstracts ***

Psychological Abstracts and PsycLit ***

Readers' Guide to Periodical Literature ***

Social Sciences Index/Abstracts ***

Sociological Abstracts ***

SPORTdiscus ***

Hands-on Exercises for Sports and Leisure Resources

The research questions that follow are simply a listing. Detailed instructions for the trainees will be included only on the accompanying disk. The reason is for the convenience of the librarians who use these exercises; they can easily be customized from the disk version. Two examples are included in this chapter to demonstrate how they have been set up as worksheets.

- Find something on the prevention of shin splints.

- What are some criteria to consider when purchasing a good pair of walking shoes?

- What cities are planning to open new baseball arenas in 1999? What are the costs and the seating capacities of these stadiums?

- When was Tiger Woods born?

- When was the Borg-Warner Trophy first awarded, and to whom?

- When did Chris Evert retire from tennis? Whom did she marry the second time? What was his profession?

- From what kind of family did Evander Holyfield come?

- Describe Evander Holyfield's attitude in the boxing ring?

- What was Picabo Street's philosophy toward the female body?

- How many basketball championships did John Wooden win during his career?

- Who was the person who bowled a perfect score? How was it attained?

- Identify the woman who shattered the world speed record in the 100-meter dash. When did this occur?

- How well do cities fare when the decision is made to put up large new sports arenas?

- Where can a patron find out a source that tells about the beginnings of ESPN?

- What was the impact of the case Pittsburgh Athletic Company v. KQV Broadcasting Company? When was this case decided?

- Where can a patron find the rules of 500 Rum and Gin Rummy card games?

- Describe hypoxia and its effects on athletes. Whom does it affect?

- Where did the phrase "on deck" come from? What does it mean?

- Can a golfer adjust a "lie" to his/her advantage?

- How do anabolic steroids affect women athletes?

- What is tai chi? Is tai chi for everyone?

- I would like to know how to play Solitaire. Where do I look for rules?

- Where could I find suggestions for games to use with the family when traveling?

NAME...

Sports and Leisure Resources Exercise

*Find something on the prevention of **shin splints**.*

Step 1   Search *Readers' Guide* and *Periodical Abstracts* (or other electronic periodical index available in your library) to see where there might be information on this topic.

Compare your experience in using these two sources.

Step 2   Does *Readers' Guide* give you help in looking up information?

What kind of help?

Step 3   In *Periodical Abstracts* (or other database you have selected) searches are often done with keywords. Was this method effective for this question?

Describe your results.

Sports and Leisure Resources Exercise

When was Tiger Woods born?

Step 1   What kinds of resources would you consider using to find this information?

List the categories.

Step 2   List three possible sources where this information could be found.

Step. 3   How did you locate the information within each source?

Document your response.

Tests and Measurements

Michael C. McGuire
Head of Reference Services
University of Maine at Farmington

Katherine Furlong
User Education and Electronic Resources Librarian
University of Maine at Farmington

Introduction

Researchers use educational and psychological tests for a variety of purposes. Scales, inventories, and tests are frequently used in educational and psychological assessments and experiments. As these tests are basic to the fields, the ability to identify and review them is crucial. Library workers need to have a basic working comprehension of these practices and to be familiar with key reference resources. This training session presents an overview of common resources, and will give you some hands-on experience in using basic reference tools.

Testing and measuring are very basic practices in education and psychology. Scales, inventories, and tests are frequently used in psychological and educational assessments and experiments. The ability to identify appropriate instruments, and in many cases read reviews of them, is very valuable to these researchers.

Circumstances for the Instruction

It's the first day of your new job on the reference desk at a small college. Nervously, but with a sense of pride, you wait for your First Reference Question. A student, wearing scruffy Doc Martens and sporting an attitude approaches the desk. Remembering your training you take a deep breath, stand up, lean forward, smile and ask in a clear, calm voice, "May I help you? "Yes," the student replies. "My professor told me I have to use Buros to complete my assignment. Where can I find Buros?" Puzzled, you try to remember if any of the reference books you've seen would have information on small equine pack animals. With a slight hesitation, and an apologetic air, you ask "Burros?"
"No, Buros."
"Donkeys?"
"What did you call me?"

With a sense of doom, you know your first day could be your last.

Eventually, painfully, you finally discover that the student needs the *Mental Measurements Yearbook,* a classic series on psychological and educational testing started by the now deceased Oscar Buros. You never did like tests.

Test anxiety is real, as is the anxiety experienced at reference desks when patrons are seeking information on educational tests and measurements. Finding quality reviews and evaluations of tests, many of which are never published and are used for research purposes only, can be challenging at best. Thankfully, there are some very useful reference resources to expedite the process.

This training session presents an overview of common resources, and will give you some hands-on experience in using basic reference tools.

Components of the Instruction and Training

Below are points that you should consider as you plan and prepare for an instruction session.

- Instructors should be experienced and knowledgeable about information resources that cover tests and measurements.
- Reserve the library's electronic teaching center for your presentations. If one is not available, reserve a library classroom.
- Ideally, the session should include an LCD panel, overhead projector, and a sufficient number of workstations to let participants engage in hands-on activities.
- Make sure all software is loaded and working on the demo computer.
- Make bookmarks for Web sites you will use. Emphasize that all information is **NOT** on the Web; effective reference work requires skill in using BOTH print and electronic information sources.
- Spend some time in preparing your lesson plans, decide what the instructional goals will be and write the instructional objectives.
- Decide how to follow through and make an evaluation of the training's effectiveness.
- Photocopy or create any materials that will be used—handouts, worksheets, and transparencies. You may wish to design a Web page for the training.
- Select examples of tests and measurements resources to discuss. You may decide to use earlier editions of titles so reference work won't be hampered because the latest editions have been taken from the ready-reference collection.
- Discuss the concepts of keyword and subject searching.
- Discuss and show participants, perhaps on the overhead, how to search for key Library of Congress Subject Headings (or Sears if that is more appropriate). There are many subject headings for tests and measurements. Selected examples are listed in the section below: Searching the Catalog.

Goals and Objectives

This session was designed to familiarize new reference workers with standard reference resources covering all aspects of tests and measurements.

The hands-on exercises included at the end of the lesson will allow participants to immediately apply their new knowledge using real-life reference questions. You may wish to develop an evaluation form to gauge your effectiveness as an instructor and the participants' comprehension.

Preparing Yourself

Reference resources are best learned through use. There are many more resources discussed in this chapter than can realistically be covered in any single training session. It is important to include those available and frequently used in your library. Remember that the hands-on exercises require that participants use the resources. Feel free to edit or customize the questions so they may be answered by resources in your library.

We have attempted to include a variety of resources, both print and electronic. It is important to include a realistic mix in your training. The exercises may be used by groups, or by participants working individually. When we train new staff and participants at the University of Maine at Farmington, we generally prefer to talk about and demonstrate resources in context; going to the reference area to discuss reference books, and the index shelves to discuss indexes.

You may wish to reproduce the Tests and Measurements handout included in this chapter. It is also on the disk so you can modify it to include local call number and location information. Last, but certainly not least, make sure to study the resources yourself. Cramming never really works. It will take time to familiarize yourself with any resources you may not use on a regular basis.

Background & Research Challenges

Educational vs. Psychological Testing

The areas of psychological testing and educational testing naturally blur, since both deal with intelligence and the workings of the mind. Generally, educational testing will deal more with aptitude and class placement. A teacher or school will administer tests to find out how much imparted knowledge participants retain. Tests will also be used to determine if a student has any special needs or learning difficulties that are not readily apparent. Psychological tests are used by many different organizations for a wide range of purposes from pure behavioral research to evaluating a current or potential employee's fitness for a task.

Searching the Catalog

The list below includes only a few suggested subject headings, all taken from the *Library of Congress Subject Headings*, 20th edition. Not surprisingly, the *LCSH* can be somewhat convoluted, so it is worthwhile to look at the volumes (or database, should you be so blessed) for scope notes and related terms.

Selected headings used for Educational Testing

Educational tests and measurements

Learning disabilities—Diagnosis

Participants—Rating of

> (This heading is used for works on evaluating participants on their total performance including "academic achievement, behavior, attitudes, interests, motivation, participation, etc.")

Selected headings used for Psychological Testing
> Psychological tests
> Psychological tests for children
> —Psychological testing
>> (A subdivision to be used with ethnic groups or other groups or classes of people.)

Finding the Tests

One of the biggest challenges to handling reference questions relating to tests and measurements is finding the actual tests. In academic institutions, an office of Testing and Measurements or the Education or Psychology Departments may be good resources. You can also check with your city (county, state) department of Mental Health. Frequently the best access to these primary materials is outside of your library.

Reference Resources for Tests & Measurements

Those sources that are also in electronic format (CD-ROM, Internet subscription) will be marked with a triple asterisk ***. The resources are arranged in the following categories in this chapter:
> Bibliographies
> Dictionaries and Encyclopedias
> Handbooks and Textbooks
> Indexes and Abstracts
> Critiques and Reviews
> Introductory Readings

Bibliographies

The ETS Test Collection Catalog, 1993–
This title serves as an index to the Educational Testing Service collection, *Tests in Microfiche*, 1975–1997. It is no longer published. Volume 1 of the *Catalog* covers achievement tests and measurement devices while Volume 2 covers vocational tests and measurement devises. Later volumes are scheduled to cover aptitude, attitude, and personality tests.

Test Construction: A Bibliography of Selected Resources. 1988.
More than 2,700 books, reports, journal articles, dissertations, and *ERIC* documents are cited in this title. The citations are arranged by test type; there are no annotations but author and subject indexes are available.

Additional specialized and general bibliographic sources are:
> *Bibliographic Index*
> *A Guide to 100 Tests for Special Education* (1996)
> *Measures for Psychological Assessment: A Guide to 3,000 Original Sources and Their Applications* (1975)
> *Working Bibliography on Behavioral and Emotional Disorders and Assessment Instruments in Mental Retardation* (1996)

Dictionaries and Encyclopedias

Encyclopedia of Educational Research. 1992 ed.
In addition to a wide range of referenced introductory essays on testing, test construction and the testing industry, this 4-volume encyclopedia has a useful appendix on "Doing Library Research in Education."

Encyclopedia of Psychology. 1994 ed.
This standard work in four volumes has excellent entries covering testing, as well as articles under the names of certain well-known tests. It is a good resource for background and methodology, with references for further information.

The International Encyclopedia of Education. 1994 ed.
This 12-volume set with over 1,000 entries provides an international perspective on all aspects of education. Extensive indexes and bibliographies are included.

The International Encyclopedia of Educational Evaluation. 1990.
Over 150 articles are included that cover significant topics in educational evaluation.

The Oxford Companion to the Mind. 1987.
A dictionary of psychology and philosophy and yet something in between, this work aims to cover all aspects of thinking, consciousness, and physiology of the brain.

A Critical Dictionary of Educational Concepts. 1990 ed.
This is an overview of ideas in educational theory and practice, including assessment and measurement.

Evaluation Thesaurus. 1991 ed.
A cross-disciplinary overview of all aspects of evaluation is provided.

Most general encyclopedias (print or electronic) will provide basic coverage of psychological and educational tests and measurements. They may also provide biographical information on key historic figures. Never underestimate the power of *Encyclopaedia Britannica*.

Handbooks and Textbooks

Not all of the following tools are strictly reference works, although they may prove useful in answering reference questions.

Assessment of Children and Youth. 1998.
This textbook provides a "fundamental understanding of the traditional and contemporary assessment of children and youth."—*Pref.* The online web site is of particular interest—http://longman.awl.com/AssessNet

The Blackwell Handbook of Education. 1995.
This Blackwell title is an alphabetical guide to all aspects of education from a British perspective.

Diagnostic and Statistical Manual of Mental Disorders. 1999.
Mental health practitioners, participants, and anyone interested in mental health use this source. It defines symptoms to aid diagnosis of mental disorders as well as describing the disorder. Particular attention should be paid to the introductory sections. The section includes cautions on using the diagnostic aspects of the work; one needs to remember the variety of human reactions, combinations of symptoms, etc.

A Handbook for Data Analysis in the Behavioral Sciences: Statistical Issues. 1993.
A Handbook for Data Analysis in the Behavioral Sciences: Methodological Issues. 1993.
These two volumes are useful for determining how data collected during tests and measurements is used and abused.

Handbook of Family Measurement Techniques. 1990.
About 1,000 instruments have been organized according to five categories. Page-long entries include a brief description of the variables measured, the instrument's content and procedures, reliability and validity, as well as availability.

Handbook of Psychological and Educational Assessment of Children. 1990.
This 2-volume set provides a review of a wide range of assessment instruments. Volume 1 covers intelligence and achievement tests and Volume 2 covers personality, behavior, and social skills tests.

Handbook of Psychological Assessment. 1997 ed.
This title is a reference guide and instructional text for psychological assessment. It includes a broad overview of assessment combined with in-depth coverage of specific tools.

Major Psychological Assessment Instruments. 1996 ed.
A useful overview of the assessment process is provided with in-depth analysis of major instruments. Excellent references for further research are included.

Measures of Personality and Social Psychological Attitudes. 1991 ed.
This title focuses on effective instruments for measuring attitudes and opinions. A sample, and in some cases the entire instrument, is reproduced. An essay describes the intent, reliability, and validity of the particular test.

Psychological Testing. 1997 ed.
Besides the tests, this title includes a lengthy section of bibliographical references and an index.

Indexes and Abstracts—Print and Electronic

Buros Institute of Mental Measurements ***
http://www.unl.edu/buros/
The web site contains an online index to the *Mental Measurements Yearbook*, starting with the ninth edition or thereabouts. It also provides links to test locators and versions of the *ERIC* database.

Current Index to Journals in Education (CIJE), 1969– (annual cumulations) ***
CIJE is an index, with brief abstracts, to current periodical literature in education and is used by faculty and participants at all levels. It covers articles published in about 800 educational and education-related journals.

Education Index, 1932– (annual cumulations) **
The *Education Index*, published by H.W. Wilson, is a cumulative index to about 300 education periodicals in the English language; selected yearbooks, monographs, and government publications are included. The index is arranged by subject headings and by author in dictionary format.

ERIC ***
http://Hericae.net/
ERIC is an educational index containing bibliographic citations to journal articles published in the literature, and to *ERIC* documents, which includes information that is not indexed elsewhere. The abstracted literature is distributed though print two titles: *Current Index to Journals in Education* and *Resources in Education.*

Health and Psychosocial Instruments (HAPI) (semiannual updates) ***
HAPI is a CD-ROM database that is designed to help identify measurement tests used in health, psychosocial sciences, organizational behavior, and library and information sciences. It provides source, abstracts, and reviewer(s) when applicable.

PsycLit/PsycInfo ***
The electronic versions of *Psychological Abstracts* contain citations for journal articles, books, book chapters, and dissertations. Recent versions of these products (as of 1998) integrate monograph records with serials records. Previously, books and book chapters were presented as a separate subset of the overall database. These same updates now make information dating back to 1887 (yes, that is 1887, not 1987) available, although not all libraries may have purchased this full data set.

Psychological Abstracts, 1927– ***
This print index includes not only journal literature but also books and book chapter citations. It is an especially good resource for reports on original research in psychology. Literature of related areas is also included: anthropology, biology, education, medicine, social work, and sociology.

See http://www.apa.org/psycinfo/compare.html for a comparison of coverage of each of the above two titles.

Resources in Education (RIE), v.10, 1975– (annual cumulations) ***
RIE is a monthly abstract journal that announces recent report literature related to the field of education. This title supersedes *Research in Education* and continues the numbering. Reports of current research findings, project and technical reports, speeches, and unpublished manuscripts are abstracted, indexed, and microfiched for distribution to subscribers. Some books are abstracted and dissertations are cited.

Tests: a Comprehensive Reference for Assessments in Psychology, Education and Business, 1983–
A broad listing of tests, it is grouped according to the areas listed in the title. Other important information is also listed, such as publisher, purpose, and a brief description of the test. It does not attempt to review or evaluate tests.

Tests in Print, 1961–
Tests in Print (TIP) and the *Mental Measurement Yearbook (MMY)* are companion tools produced by the same organization. There are, however, some notable differences. *Tests in Print* is more comprehensive. A test need only be in print at the time of publication. *Tests in Print* does not include reviews. This resource may also be used as a comprehensive index to all the *MMY*s in print up to the date of publication of the latest *TIP*.

Other sources of tests include:
Assessing Participants with Special Needs: A Sourcebook
Biological Abstracts ***
Designing Tests for Evaluating Participants' Achievement
Dissertation Abstracts International
Educational Testing for the Millions; What Tests Really Mean for Your Child
Educational Testing: Issues and Applications
ETS Test Collection (on microfiche)
Facts on File Dictionary of Education
Index to Tests Used in Educational Dissertations
Medline ***
Periodical Abstracts ***
Social Work Abstracts ***
Tests and Measurements in Child Development

Critiques and Reviews
The Mental Measurements Yearbook, 1938– ***
This monumental collection is also known as "Buros" for the original compiler, Oscar Krisen Buros. It contains a wealth of information about each reviewed test, including author, publisher, format, and purpose for the tests. Each review is signed and followed by the reviewer's bibliography. *MMY* is essentially an encyclopedia of reviews of commercially available (as of the date of publication of the *MMY*) tests and measure-

ments that are new or have been revised, or have received at least 20 references in the literature since the previous edition of the *MMY* was published. The arrangement is alphabetical by test title. A subject index is included, a useful feature if an exact test title is not known. The publishers make as a goal a new edition every two years with a supplement released between editions. The online version is updated monthly.

Test Critiques, 1991–
This title contains basic information as well as evaluations of tests. Review articles are signed and most include a bibliography.

Introductory Readings

Modern Educational Measurement: A Practitioner's Perspective (1990)
Psychological Testing (1997 ed.)

Tests and Measurements Handout

A handout that was developed for this training session is found on the following page. It has also been included on the accompanying disk for your convenience. You may wish to reproduce it and/or modify it to include local call number and location information.

Tests and Measurements

Important Reference Materials:

The Mental Measurements Yearbook
Personality Tests and Reviews
Reading Tests and Reviews
A Guide to 100 Tests for Special Education
*Tests: A Comprehensive Reference for Assessments in Psychology, Education and
    Business*
Test Critiques

Searching Databases

These are a few suggested headings to get you started. Use the thesaurus that
goes with the database for additional terms. With any database, also try searching
the name of the test in question.

Library of Congress Subject Headings
> Educational Tests and Measurements
> Learning Disabilities—Diagnosis Psychological Tests
> Special Education

ERIC Descriptors
> Educational Assessment
> Educational Diagnosis
> Evaluation

PsycInfo Descriptors
> Intelligence Measures
> Cognitive Assessment
> Educational Placement
> Ability Grouping

Web sites

Buros Institute of Mental Measurements   http://www.unl.edu/buros/
AssessNet: Assessment of Children and Youth   http://longman.awl.com/assessnet
The Federal Resource Center for Special Education   http://www.dssc.org/frc/frc1.htm

---

Michael C. McGuire, University of Maine at Farmington 2/99

Hands-on Exercises

The exercises below are set up on the disk with detailed instructions for participants; the first two are included in the text as examples of how the worksheets are constructed. Each participant will have a set of three questions to answer. For your convenience, you may print each set as a separate page for easy distribution, and/or customize them to fit the needs of your situation.

Each worksheet is constructed to require the participants to make hands-on use of *The Mental Measurements Yearbook* or *Test Critiques,* another reference work, (generally an encyclopedia or dictionary) and a bibliography or database. Participants should be strongly encouraged to use *ERIC* or *PsycLit,* if available, however, the questions are answerable with a good general periodical index such as *The Readers' Guide to Periodical Literature* or *Expanded Academic ASAP.*

1. A patron is looking for a review of the management test called the MSI. Use the *Mental Measurements Yearbook* or *Test Critiques* to find the name of the test and current reviews. How many tests use the MSI acronym?

2. Use a psychological or educational dictionary to define *goal-based evaluation.*

3. Using *ERIC* or another database, find a recent article critiquing goal-based evaluation.

*****

1. When was the Marital Attitudes Evaluation (A4A TE) first developed? Use the *Mental Measurements Yearbook* or *Test Critiques* to find the answer.

2. Does the concept of *laissez-faire* have anything to do with evaluation?

3. Using *PsycINFO* or another database, try to locate a longitudinal study on the prevention of marital distress.

*****

1. Use the *Mental Measurements Yearbook* or *Test Critiques* to find a review of the 1957 edition of the *California Reading Test.* What is the most recent edition of the test that you can find?

2. In what year was the report *A Nation at Risk* published? What impact did the report have on education in the United States?

3. Using *ERIC* or *PsycINFO*, find an article written in the past three years critiquing the report, *A Nation at Risk.*

1. How do educators test for giftedness? Use the subject indexes of the *Mental Measurements Yearbook* or *Test Critiques* to find a test for giftedness.

2. In education, what is the definition of giftedness?

3. A faculty member has a partial citation for a 1997 article discussing the evaluation of gifted children by an author named Cameron. Use *PsycINFO* or another database to find the full citation.

*****

1. Is there an inventory to test for eating disorders? Use the *Mental Measurements Yearbook* or *Test Critiques* to look for an inventory.

2. Use a psychological dictionary or encyclopedia to find a definition of anorexia nervosa.

3. Has there ever been a case of anorexia by proxy? Use *PsycINFO* or another database to try to find the answer.

*****

1. A student is writing a paper on ADD and ADHD. What do the acronyms stand for? Which is the preferred term in psychology? In education?

2. Are there any tests available to assist teachers and psychologists in determining the severity of ADD or ADHD based on displayed behaviors? Use the *Mental Measurements Yearbook* or *Test Critiques* to find a measurement tool.

3. The student would like to find the best course of treatment for ADD or ADHD. Using an index find articles on treatment.

*****

1. Use the *Mental Measurements Yearbook* or *Test Critiques* to find a test that can help plan the reading and math curriculum for pre-grade 1 participants.

2. A student is writing a paper arguing that Kindergarten should be eliminated. Are there any scholarly articles (written by education researchers) that support this theory? Use *ERIC, Education Index* or another database to search for articles.

3. What is the definition of Educational Preparedness?

1. What is stress resiliency? Use the *Mental Measurements Yearbook* or *Test Critiques* to find a test for stress resiliency.

2. A faculty member is requesting information for a graduate student exhibiting signs of test anxiety. Find a current definition of test anxiety.

3. The faculty member wants to know how to measure the severity of test anxiety. Have any current, scholarly articles been written on how to test for "test anxiety?" Use *PsycINFO* or another database to find out.

Exercise—Tests & Measurements

Using the reference tools discussed in class, answer the three reference questions listed below. You may need to consult more than one resource for each question.

No. 1   A patron is looking for a review of the **management test called the MSI**.

Use the *Mental Measurements Yearbook* or *Test Critiques* to find the name of the test and current reviews.

How many tests use the MSI acronym?

Resource(s) used:

What is the full name of the MSI management test?

How many other tests use the MSI acronym?

No. 2   Use a psychological or educational dictionary to define **goal-based evaluation**.

Dictionary used:

Definition:

No. 3   Using *ERIC* or another database, find a recent **article critiquing goal-based evaluation**.

Database used:

Citation:

Exercise—Tests & Measurements

Using the reference tools discussed in class, answer the three reference questions listed below. You may need to consult more than one resource for each question.

No. 1   When was the **Marital ATtitudes Evaluation** (MATE) was first developed? Use *Test Critiques* to find the answer.

    Test Critiques volume: page:

    Answer:

    What does the *Mental Measurements Yearbook* have to say about the MATE's effectiveness?

    MMY edition:

    Answer:

No. 2   Does the **concept of laissez-faire** have anything to do with evaluation? Use a dictionary of educational or psychological evaluation to find an answer.

    Dictionary used:

No. 3   Using *PsycINFO* or another database, locate a longitudinal study on the prevention of marital distress.

Database used:

Answer:

Notes:

Treaties

TERRI D. HAWKINS
Database Librarian
SAILOR, MARYLAND'S ONLINE PUBLIC INFORMATION NETWORK

Introduction

What Is a Treaty?

A treaty is an international law or agreement between two or more nations. It may be a political treaty – one that ends conflict or territorial disputes, or a commercial treaty – one that deals with tariffs, trade, and tourism. Researching treaties is not easy – there are many specialized indexes and guides necessary for locating the text of treaties. Users researching treaties often require the assistance of a reference librarian through the entire research process. This process can be complex and time consuming especially if the librarians are unfamiliar with the treaty resources available at their library. For this reason it is important to train reference staff in the use of the available materials as well as provide information about other local libraries that may have specialized treaty collections.

Treaty Nomenclature

Treaties may be called several different names including agreements, acts, conventions, protocols, accords, pact, declaration, charters, covenants, constitutions for international organization, and memorandums of understanding. These different names usually have no legal significance.

What Is the Patron Seeking?

Users asking about treaties may be looking for a variety of information and it is important to determine exactly what they need in the reference interview. The librarian needs to be aware of all of the different aspects of a treaty, all the different issues a patron may have in mind when asking for help in "finding a treaty." By asking several preliminary questions, the librarian can provide the best possible assistance to the patron. Some questions for which users may seek answers include:

- Is the U.S. a party to the treaty?
- Is the treaty bilateral (between two parties) or multilateral (between several parties)?
- What countries signed the treaty?
- How old is the treaty?
- Is the treaty still in force?
- Are there amendments to the treaty?
- Where is the full text of the treaty?
- Does such a treaty even exist?
- Is there commentary and analysis available about the treaty?

When users ask about a treaty, they may be seeking answers to one or all of these questions and it is important to determine the level of information they seek before beginning the research process. By gathering a few details about the nature of a treaty request, the librarian can narrow down the research focus to a limited set of research tools. For example, a patron may only need to find the names of the signing countries and not need the full text. This information could be found in a variety of indexes and is less time consuming than locating the full text, so it is important for the librarian to determine the level of information needed by the patron.

A special note on treaties between the United States and Native Americans:
Treaties between the United States and Native Americans have, for the most part, been excluded from collections of U.S. treaties and other international agreements. See the section in this chapter on **treaties by subject** for a few resources and some hints for finding these types of treaties.

Components of the Instruction and Training

With so many specialized resources required when researching treaties, it is recommended that three different training sessions take place:
1. one for U.S. treaties,
2. one for international treaties, and
3. a third for electronic and subject specific treaty resources.
However, if your library has a small collection, one session may suffice.

Getting Started
➢ Prepare a handout with the title, call number and location of all treaty resources available in your library, including indexes and full text resources. This list should be divided into the three categories of training: U.S. treaties, international treaties, and electronic and subject specific treaties. You may also wish to prepare a handout for general resources, such as almanacs, encyclopedias and yearbooks.
➢ Prepare a handout and/or web site listing common citations of basic treaty collections. This list should include the following (even if your library does not have these resources):
  • Bevans (*Treaties and Other International Agreements of the United States of America, 1776–1949*, compiled by Charles I. Bevans)
  • CTS (*Current Treaty Series*)
  • *KAV* (Treaties and agreements of the U.S. not yet published in *TIAS* but appearing in indexes and/or microfiche sets compiled and edited by Igor I. Kavass)
  • *LNTS* or *LTS* (*League of Nations Treaty Series*)
  • *STAT* (*United States Statutes at Large*)
  • *TIAS* (*Treaties and Other International Acts Series*)
  • *TIF* (*Treaties in Force*)
  • *UNTS* (*United Nations Treaty Series*)
  • *UST* (*United States Treaties and Other International Agreements Series*)

➤ Prepare a handout with the address and phone number for local Federal Depository Libraries (FDLP) and your Regional Federal Depository Library. *GPO Access*— http://www.access.gpo.gov—allows you to search for FDLP libraries by state or area code. Keep copies at the reference desk.

➤ Determine the best physical space for holding your training session. For U.S. session this may be in the Government Documents Department. For International, the best place may be the Reference Department or the Government Documents Department, depending on your collection. For electronic resources and treaties by subjects, reserve an electronic classroom.

U.S. Treaties Session

➤ Gather a selection of resources to display.

➤ Provide an overview/introduction about what treaties are, the different names they are called, and what information users may be seeking when asking for help finding a treaty.

➤ Discuss the basics of your library's collection for U.S. treaties. Is it limited or broad in scope, in what department are these resources located, etc?

➤ Offer suggestions for other local libraries to go to for U.S. treaty information if your collection is limited. Prepare a handout listing local depository library information.

➤ Discuss Library of Congress subject headings that can be used in your catalog to find indexes and treaty collections. If necessary demonstrate how to search for subject headings in your library's catalog. Some subject headings for U.S. treaties include:
  - Alliances
  - Commercial Treaties
  - Treaties—Indexes
  - Treaties—Collections
  - Treaty-making power—United States
  - United States—Foreign Relations
  - United States—Foreign Relations—[country name]
  - United States—Foreign Relations—date
  - United States—Foreign Relations—Treaties
  - United States—Foreign Relations—Treaties—Indexes
  - United States—Politics and Government
  - [country name]—Foreign Relations—United States

➤ Now you are ready to discuss your library's U.S. treaty resources in depth. Describe each available resource and how to use it.

➤ After discussing the resources your library does have, it is a good idea to discuss the resources your library does not have. If your collection does not provide the answer to users' questions, the librarian should be able to point them to a source in another library where they can get an answer. In order to accomplish this, the librarian needs to know something about those other resources and develop some search strategies to pass along to the patron.

International Treaties Session

➢ Gather a selection of resources to display.

➢ If it has been a long time since the previous training session, you may wish to reiterate the basic information about what treaties are, the different names they are called, and what information users may be seeking when asking for help finding a treaty.

➢ Discuss the basics of your library's collection for international treaties. Is it limited or broad in scope, in what department are these resources located, etc?

➢ Offer suggestions for other local libraries to go to for international treaty information if your collection is limited. Many Federal Depository Libraries maintain extensive international government documents collections.

➢ Discuss Library of Congress subject headings that can be used in your catalog to find indexes and treaty collections. If necessary demonstrate how to search for subject headings in your library's catalog. Some subject headings for international treaties include:
  - Treaties—Indexes
  - Treaties—Collections
  - Treaties—[country name]—Foreign Relations
  - Treaties—Bibliography
  - Treaty-making power—[country name]
  - United Nations—Indexes
  - [country name]—Foreign Relations
  - [country name]—Foreign Relations—Treaties
  - [country name]—Politics and Government
  - [country name]—Treaties, etc.

➢ Now you are ready to discuss your library's international treaty resources in depth. Describe each available resource and how to use it.

➢ After discussing the resources your library does have, it is a good idea to discuss the resources your library does not have. If your collection does not provide the answer to users' questions, the librarian should be able to point them to a source in another library where they can get an answer. In order to accomplish this, the librarian needs to know something about those other resources and develop some search strategies to pass along to the patron.

Electronic and Subject Treaties Session

➢ Gather a selection of resources to display. For electronic resources, bookmark different sites on the computer that will be used for the training session.

➢ If it has been a long time since the previous training session, you may wish to reiterate the basic information about what treaties are, the different names they are called, and what information users may be seeking when asking for help finding a treaty.

➢ Discuss basics of your library's collection for electronic treaty resources – is it limited or broad in scope, in what department are these resources located, etc.

- Discuss basics of your library's collection for subject specific treaties. Is it limited or broad in scope, in what department are these resources located, etc?
- Offer suggestions for other local libraries to go to for electronic resources and subject specific treaty information if your collection is limited. For example, a human rights library would be an excellent subject specific resource.
- For electronic resources, there are no consistent subject headings and quite often, electronic resources are not cataloged. For these resources it is best to prepare a handout listing the electronic resources available in your library. Also, a handout on different search engines and search strategies can be helpful.
- Discuss Library of Congress subject headings that can be used in your catalog to find treaties by subject. For specific subject areas, the patron will have more luck finding a book or two in the library collection which may include treaties. If necessary, demonstrate how to search for subject headings in your library's catalog. Some subject areas that may have related treaties include:
  - Environmental Law (International)
  - Human Rights
  - Indians—Government relations
  - Indians of North America—Legal status, laws, etc.
  - Indians of North America—Treaties
  - Nuclear Arms Control
  - Treaties—Indexes
  - War (International law)
  - Women (International law)
  - Women—Legal status, laws, etc.
  - The subdivision "Treaties" following any Native American tribal name (example: Arapahoe Indian Treaties)
- Now you are ready to discuss your library's electronic and subject specific treaty resources in depth. Describe each resource and how to use it.
- After discussing the resources your library does have, it is a good idea to discuss the resources your library does not have. If your collection does not provide the answer to users' questions, the librarian should be able to point them to a source in another library where they can get an answer. In order to accomplish this, the librarian needs to know something about those other resources and develop some search strategies to pass along to the patron.

Selected Reference Resources for Treaties

Sources available electronically (CD-ROM, Internet subscription) will be marked with a triple asterisk ***. The resources in this chapter are arranged by the following categories:

General Resources
Almanacs and Yearbooks
Encyclopedias
Indexes and Abstracts
Treaties—United States
   Indexes, Guides, and Finding Aids
   Full Text Resources

General Resources

These general resources are intended to provide treaty resources for libraries that may not have extensive government document collections. Within these more general resources it may be possible to locate commentary and analysis of some of the major treaties, but it is unlikely you will find the full text.

Almanacs and Yearbooks

Almanac of American History. 1993 ed.
This chronological survey covers American history from 986 through 1992. It provides summary information on U.S. treaties including title, date, and purpose. This is a nice source for those looking for treaties in an historical context.

Facts on File World Political Almanac. 1995.
Chapter four of this almanac offers a list of politically significant treaties, alliances, and diplomatic agreements divided by country. Within each country, treaties are listed in chronological order from 1945 to 1994 with a brief entry including title and purpose. It includes a bibliography.

Historic Documents, 1972– (annual)
This annual publication from Congressional Quarterly Inc. includes the text of some treaties. If the patron knows the year of the treaty, simply look at the table of contents for that year's volume to determine if the text is there (or if any other documents regarding that treaty are included). There are also five-year cumulative indexes at the end of some volumes.

Encyclopedias

Encyclopedia of American Facts and Dates. 1997.
The chronological coverage of American history is from 986 through 1996. Four subject areas are displayed concurrently across the page: politics, culture, business and economics, and society. Treaties can be located by date (if known) or by the index. This is a good source for those looking for treaties in an historical context.

Encyclopedia of U.S. Foreign Relations. 1997.
Treaties may be found in this 4-volume set by name or subject. Although this reference resource will not provide the full text of a treaty, if does offer informative articles on the political situations surrounding a treaty.

Encyclopedia of the United Nations and International Agreements. 1990.
This single volume contains the text of a select number of treaties important in the history

of the United Nations. It also provides useful information on the structure of the U.N.

International Encyclopedia of Public Policy and Administration. 1998.
This 4-volume set contains entries for some of the major international treaties, with brief discussion of signing parties, entry into force, and affects of the treaty.

Oxford Companion to Politics of the World. 1993.
Brief analysis and discussion of politically significant international laws and treaties are contained in this title. Treaties are listed by title in the index. Some maps and a bibliography are included.

Worldmark Encyclopedia of the Nations. 1998.
This title provides nice summaries of major international treaties, especially in Volume 1 (United Nations). Volumes 2 through 5, covering different regions of the world, provide economic, political and social information for all the nations of the world.

Miscellaneous encyclopedias

Most encyclopedias will contain some background information on major international treaties. Looking them up by title, country, or subject should garner some basic treaty information. Examples of encyclopedias, one or two of which should be available in most academic and public libraries, include: *Americana, Britannica, Collier's, Columbia,* and *World Book.* These encyclopedias are also available in electronic format.

General Indexes and Abstracts—Print and Electronic

Try these more general indexes if the specialized resources listed below are not available in your library. These will provide citations to articles about many major treaties but will probably not assist in locating the full text. In each index or abstract service, you can look for treaties by title, country, or subject. These resources are available in both a print and electronic format.

> *America: History and Life* ***
> *Historical Abstracts* ***
> *Humanities Index* ***
> *International Political Science Abstracts* ***
> *PAIS (Public Affairs Information Service)* ***
> *Periodical Abstracts* ***
> *Readers' Guide to Periodical Literature* ***
> *Social Sciences Index* ***

Treaties—United States

Treaties in the United States must be signed by the President and ratified by the Senate. They may be bilateral or multilateral. While different indexes cover different years and publications, there are some standard citations that it is important to remember.

Most citations to official government publications will follow the pattern of providing the volume number, the publication's initials, and then the page number. For example, a citation to the Statutes at Large will look like this 17 STAT 187 where 17 is the volume number and 187 is the page number.

Other publications that follow this format include *the Executive Agreement Series (EAS)*, *Treaties and Other International Agreements of the United States of America 1776–1949* (Bevans), and *United States Treaties and Other International Agreements Series (UST)*. *Treaties and Other International Acts Series (TIAS)* and *Treaty Series (TS)* do not follow this practice since these are issued in consecutively numbered pamphlets. These are simply listed as *TIAS* 5970 or *TS* 924 where 5970 and 924 are the pamphlet numbers.

Indexes, Guides, and Finding Aids for U.S. Treaties

CIS Annual, 1970– ***
This annual publication from Congressional Information Service provides an index and abstract of congressional publications including executive reports and treaty documents. The annual is currently divided into 3 parts: Abstracts, Index, and Legislative Histories. Using the annual index (or the five-year cumulative indexes), treaties can be located by subject or title. The index will provide both the CIS abstract number and the Senate Treaty Document number. The *CIS Annual* is available electronically but only through subscription; it is part of *Congressional Universe* available from Lexis-Nexis. For more details see—www.cispubs.com.

Congressional Record Index.
This title provides a list of treaty actions or discussions in Congress, as recorded in the *Congressional Record*. It is a good source for information on recent treaties (although not the full text) and legislative history. It is also available on *GPO Access—* http://www.access.gpo.gov.

Cumulative Index to United States Treaties and Other International Agreements 1776–1949 as published in *Statutes at Large*, Malloy, Miller, Bevans, and other relevant sources (a.k.a. *United States Treaties and Other International Agreements Cumulative Index, 1776–1949*. 1975.)
This 4-volume set, compiled by Igor I. Kavass and Mark A. Michael, is one of the key references for finding the full text of U.S. treaties, both perfected and unperfected. It indexes several important sources including *TS, EAS,* and *TIAS*, plus additional documents. *UST Cumulative Index* is an ongoing supplement to this set. Volume 1 is in numerical order of *TS, EAS, TIAS,* and *AD* numbers. Volume 2 is a chronological index, Volume 3 is a country index, and Volume 4 is a subject index.

Current Treaty Index: A Cumulative Index to the United States Slip Treaties and Agreements, 1982– (semi-annual)
The title provides a list of current treaties published in *TIAS* and those not yet assigned *TIAS* numbers (these are referred to by *KAV* numbers). Entries include a brief description of the treaty and pertinent dates.

Treaties in Force; A List of Treaties and Other International Agreements of the United States, 1932– (annual)

This annual publication offers a brief summary of all U.S. treaties and agreements still in force as of January 1 of the year of the annual. Arranged in two parts (bilateral and multilateral), this list includes citations to locate the full text of the treaty.

UST Cumulative Index, 1950–1970: Cumulative Index to United States Treaties and Other International Agreements 1950–1970. 1973.

This 4-volume set is a supplement to *Cumulative Index to United States Treaties and Other International Agreements 1776–1949.* Volume 1 is in *TIAS* numerical order, Volume 2 is a chronological index, Volume 3 is a country index, and Volume 4 is a subject index.

UST Cumulative Index, 1971–1975: Cumulative Index to United States Treaties and Other International Agreements 1971–1975. 1977.

This is a supplement to both *Cumulative Index to United States Treaties and Other International Agreements 1776–1949* and the preceding title. This single volume is divided into four parts: Pt. 1 is in *TIAS* numerical order, Pt. 2 is a chronological index, Pt. 3 is a country index, and Pt. 4 is a subject index.

UST Cumulative Indexing Service, 1978–

This is a loose-leaf supplement to *Cumulative Index to United States Treaties and Other International Agreements 1776–1949* and the two preceding titles. It is cumulated every five years.

Full Text Resources for U.S. Treaties

Executive Agreement Series (EAS). 1929–1945.

The full text of U.S. treaties and agreements published from 1929 through 1945 is included. It combined with *TS* to form *Treaties and Other International Acts Series (TIAS)* in 1945.

Senate Treaty Document Series, 1982–

The series was called *Senate Executive Documents* until the 97th Congress, 1981. The Senate issues a treaty document when the President asks them to ratify a treaty or convention. The treaty document (or executive document) usually includes the committee recommendations and the text of the treaty. It is indexed in *CIS Annual****.

Treaties and Other International Acts Series (TIAS), 1950– (#1501–)

This consecutively numbered series of individual pamphlets provide the full text of U.S. treaties before they are published in *UST*. The text appears in both the authentic language of the treaty and English. Often referred to as "slip" treaties, the individual pamphlets are usually discarded when the treaty appears in the bound *UST* (and is assigned a *UST* number). This series replaced both *TS* and *EAS*.

Treaties and Other International Agreements of the United States of America, 1776–1949. 1975.
This 13-volume set, cited as "Bevans" for the compiler Charles I. Bevans, is a major resource for the full text of U.S. treaties from 1776 to 1949. Volumes 1 through 4 offer multilateral treaties (v.1 1776–1917, v. 2 1918–1930, v. 3 1931–1945, and v. 4 1946–1949). Volumes 5 through 12 are bilateral agreements arranged alphabetically by country (v. 5 Afghanistan–Burma, v. 6 Canada–Czechoslovakia, v. 7 Denmark–France, v. 8 Germany–Iran, v. 9 Iraq–Muscat, v. 10 Nepal–Peru, v. 11 Philippines–United Arab Republic, and v. 12 United Kingdom–Zanzibar). Volume 13 is a general index.

Treaties, Conventions, International Acts, Protocols, and Agreements between the United States of America and Other Powers, 1910–1938.
This 4-volume set covers 1776 through 1937. It provides treaty texts in English with citations to the official text in *STAT* and *TS*. These treaties are listed in chronological order. Volume 4 contains both an alphabetical and a chronological index.

Treaty Series (TS). 1800's–1945.
This consecutively numbered pamphlet series began as an unnumbered series in the 1800's. It combined with *EAS* to form *Treaties and Other International Acts Series (TIAS)* in 1945.

United States Statutes at Large (STAT). pre-1950.
The full texts of U.S. treaties were printed in the *Statutes at Large* until 1950. This set is arranged chronologically. Native American treaties were included through Volume 16, although not comprehensively. While this series is still published today, it no longer includes treaties. For post-1950 treaties, see *TIAS* and *UST*.

United States Treaties and Other International Agreements (UST), 1950–
After appearing in the *TIAS* "slip" form, the full text of U.S. treaties are published in the bound volumes of this chronological series. Treaties appear in both their authentic language and English. Each volume lists the documents contained therein in *TIAS* order. Each volume has a subject index.

United States Treaties and Other International Agreements Current Service (a.k.a. Hein's).
A good source for the full text of recent treaties, it is more timely than *TIAS* and *UST*. It provides the full text of unreleased international treaties, agreements, and acts. The titles are listed by *KAV* numbers and are indexed in the *Current Treaty Index*.

Unperfected Treaties of the United States of America 1776–1976. 1976.
This 9-volume set is an excellent resource for unperfected/unratified U.S. treaties. An index is included.

Indexes, Guides, & Finding Aids for International Treaties

These resources are used for locating bilateral and multilateral international treaties in which the U.S. may or may not be a party. While different indexes cover different years and publications, there are some standard citations that it is important to remember. Most citations to official government publications will follow the pattern of providing the volume number, the publication's initials, and then the page number. For example, a citation to the *United Nations Treaty Series* will appear as 593 *UNTS* 261 where 593 is the volume number and 261 is the page number. Other publications that follow this format include the *League of Nations Treaty Series (LNTS)*.

Consolidated Treaty Series, Index-Guide (CTS), 1969–
This treaty series is indexed by party and by country. It is arranged chronologically within each country entry. It includes citations to *Consolidated Treaty Series (CTS)* volume and page number. There is no subject index.

Index to Multilateral Treaties: A Chronological List of Multi-Party International Agreements from the 16th Century through 1963 with Citations to Their Text. 1965.
This volume provides citations to multilateral treaties dating from 1596 to 1963. Indexed by region and subject, it includes the date and place of signature along with sources for the full text. This index is especially helpful in locating obscure treaties.

Multilateral Treaties: Index and Current Status. 1984.
A chronological index for multilateral treaties, this source includes a keyword and subject index and a cumulative supplement. Citations include signatures, date of entry into force, legal title, reservations, and location of full text. This is a comprehensive, current index kept up-to-date with periodic supplements.

Multilateral Treaties Deposited with the Secretary General, 1981–
The former title was *Multilateral Treaties in Respect of which the Secretary-General Performs Depositary Functions. List of Signatures, Ratifications, Accessions, etc.* It is also available on the Internet—http://www.un.org/Depts/Treaty. Information on current status, amendments, reservations, ratification, and location of full text for all multilateral treaties deposited with the UN Secretary-General since 1946 is provided. It also has a section on League of Nations treaties.

Treaty Series (League of Nations), Index. 1927–1946.
This is a 9-volume set of cumulative indexes for the *League of Nations Treaty Series.* The numbered list includes *LTS (LNTS)* citation, type of treaty (bilateral or multilateral), title, language(s), signing countries, dates of signature and ratification, etc.

United Nations Treaty Series (UNTS) Cumulative Index, 1956–
This is the cumulative index to the *United Nations Treaty Series.* It includes *UNTS*

citation, type of treaty (bilateral or multilateral), title, language(s), signatures, date(s) of signature(s) and ratification, etc.

World Treaty Index. 1983.
This 5-volume set covers the period from 1900 to 1980. Indexed by date, keyword and party, it provides a list of all signing parties and citation to the full text of each treaty.

Full Text Resources for International Treaties

Consolidated Treaty Series (CTS), 1969–
This comprehensive 231 volume series covers from 1648 to 1918 and includes the full text of international treaties in the authentic language, English and French. The arrangement is chronological. It is indexed in *Consolidated Treaty Series, Index-Guide.*

Current International Treaties. 1984.
This title offers the full text of major bilateral and multilateral treaties which "form the legal skeleton of so much of current international relations." The appendix is especially helpful by providing a list of multilateral instruments and the countries that signed them. Commentary and analysis in addition to the full text are provided.

International Instruments of the United Nations: A Compilation of: Agreements, Charters, Conventions, Declarations, 1945–1995. 1997.
This volume offers a collection of significant United Nations documents including some treaties. It is limited.

International Legal Materials, 1962– (bi-monthly)
This publication may include the full text or selected excerpts of major international treaties (in English) which have not yet been published in one of the official government resources. It is a good source for recent treaties.

Key Treaties of the Great Powers, 1814–1914. 1972.
This set contains the complete text of significant international treaties from 1814 through 1914. Volume 1 covers from 1814 to 1870 and Volume 2 covers from 1871 to 1914. It is arranged in chronological order; Volume 2 includes both a chronological and a general index.

Major Peace Treaties of Modern History, 1648–1967. 1967.
An excellent source for older treaties, this 4-volume set provides an extensive collection of peace treaties with English translations of many foreign treaties. All of the original spelling and geographic terms found in the original texts are maintained. It includes an index and maps.

Major Peace Treaties of Modern History, 1967–1979. 1980.
This is a supplementary volume to *Major Peace Treaties of Modern History, 1648–1967* (often catalogued as volume 5 of that set) providing the full text of peace treaties in English, from 1967 to 1979.

Treaties and Alliances of the World. 1995.
This is a nice source for commentary, analysis, and some text of treaties. It is divided
into four parts: background and origins, international organizations, regional agreements,
and transregional alliances and other informal groupings.

Treaty Series (League of Nations), 1920–1946.
The full text of over 4,800 treaties, in English, French, and the authentic language of the
treaty are included. It is continued by the United Nations Treaty Series.

United Nations Treaty Series (UNTS), 1946/47– ∗∗∗
The full text of treaties is available in English, French, and the authentic language of the
treaty. Recent treaties are not available as this series has about a 10-year lag. It continues
the *League of Nations Treaty Series.* The series is also available on the Internet at—
http://www.un.org/Depts/Treaty.

World Wide Web Resources and other Electronic Resources

When researching treaties on the Internet, it is vital to look for respectable sites with
authentic texts. When looking for the full text of a treaty, look for sites that list the legal
citation along with the full text. Often the best sites are maintained by educational or
non-profit organizations. If a site has any obvious typographical errors or misspellings it
is best to find a different site and/or a print resource.

Access UN
This Readex *United Nations Index* provides access to United Nations documents,
including some treaties, from 1966 to the present. A subscription is required.

Council of Europe Treaties
http://www.coe.fr/eng/legaltxt/treaties.htm
The treaties are organized by subject and by country. The full texts of treaties are
available in both English and French. It is limited to treaties deposited in the archives of
the Council of Europe.

Foreign Governments – Constitutions, Laws and Treaties
http://www.lib.umich.edu/libhome/Documents.center/forcons.html
While this site does not contain any full text treaties, it does provide excellent links to
other online resources. It is maintained by the Documents Librarian at the University of
Michigan.

GPO Access
http://www.access.gpo.gov/su_docs/dbsearch.html
This is a free service of the U.S. Government Printing Office. It provides electronic
access to a great deal of federal government information and publications, including some
treaties and the Congressi*onal Record.*

International Treaties

Texas A&M University Library
http://library.tamu.edu/govdocs/workshop/treaties.html
This site from Texas A&M University provides a nice series of links to other Internet resources for treaties. It is divided by subject.

Lexis-Nexis
This database of full text articles from newspapers, magazines, and legal sources, may provide access to analysis and commentary of treaties and/or the full text. Subscription is required.

Multilaterals Treaties Project at Tufts University's Fletcher School of Law and Diplomacy
http://www.tufts.edu/fletcher/multilaterals.html
This project, begun in 1992, is an ongoing project of the Fletcher School of Law & Diplomacy of Tufts University. The project provides full text access to treaties in many different subject areas including arms control, commerce, the environment, human rights, and trade. Most treaties on this site are from the last half of the 20th century but some important historical texts are also available.

Treaties in Force
http://www.acda.gov/state/
This Internet version of *Treaties in Force* is the same as the print version [1955– (annual) and 1941–1954 (irregular)]. It offers a list of current U.S. treaties still in force in **pdf** format.

United Nations Master Treaty Index on CD-ROM
This semi-annual cumulative index to the *United Nations Treaty Series* is searchable by treaty name, party, dates, descriptive text and subject. Subscription is required.

United Nations Treaty Collection
http://www.un.org/Depts/Treaty
This previously free collection includes both *Multilateral Treaties Deposited with the Secretary-General* and *United Nations Treaty Series*. The *Multilateral Treaties* are updated weekly while *UNTS* has about a 10-year lag. This online version of the print covers 1946 to the present. Subscription is required.

Washburn University School of Law Library
http://lawlib.wuacc.edu/forint/treaties/treatylist.htm
The Washburn University School of Law Library has set up an extensive alphabetical list of treaties, agreements, and conventions with links to the full text. The dates of coverage are not clear. No subscription is required.

Miscellaneous Search Engines
There are several search engines available on the Internet. Some that are especially useful when researching treaties include *Infoseek*—http://infoseek.go.com, the *Mining*

Company—http://home.minigco.com, *Northern Light*—http://www.northernlight.com, and *Yahoo*—http://www.yahoo.com. All of these can be searched using subject headings similar to the Library of Congress subject headings found in the library catalog.

Treaties by Subject

Locating treaties for certain subject areas can prove challenging. Recently, many special collections have been developed on the Internet. This section is, in many ways, a continuation of the previous electronic resource section, although some books are included. This is a limited sample of treaty by subject resources. To find additional books, try a subject search in the library catalog. To find additional web sites, see the section above on Miscellaneous Search Engines.

Compendium of International Conventions Concerning the Status of Women. 1988.
A United Nations publication, this volume offers the texts of several conventions concerning women. It includes a bibliography.

Environmental Treaties and Resource Indicators
http://sedac.ciesin.org/entri/
This site offers the full text of major international environmental treaties; the dates of coverage are not clear. There are a variety of search techniques on this site including keyword, browsing, dates, parties, and subject. There are also alphabetical and chronological lists of treaties.

Human Rights Resources
http://www.umn.edu/humanrts
This is a collection of human rights treaties and documents placed on the Internet by the Human Rights Library at the University of Minnesota. Nicely arranged and easy to use, this searchable collection includes links to other Internet resources.

Indian Affairs: Laws and Treaties. 1904.
This older volume offers a nice collection of hard-to-find Native American treaties. Published by the Government Printing Office, it may be found in a regional depository library collection or other special library.

Indian Treaties Printed by Benjamin Franklin, 1736–1762. 1938.
The title includes an introduction by Carl Van Doren and historical and bibliographical notes by Julian P. Boyd. Another historical collection of Native American treaties, this volume provides the full text of 13 treaties along with several maps and a bibliography.

Oneida Indian Nation Treaties Project
http://one-web.org/oneida/treaties.html
This site offers the full text of a limited number of treaties entered into by the Oneida Indian Nation in the 18th Century. Currently focusing on Oneida Indian Nation treaties, the site will expand to include significant treaties from other Indian Nations in the future.

Treaties between the United States and Native Americans
http://www.yale.edu/lawweb/avalon/ntreaty/ntreaty.htm
This is a searchable site with links to the full text of approximately 30 U.S./Native
American treaties completed from 1778 to 1968.

U.S. Arms Control and Armament Agency, Treaties and Agreements
http://www.acda.gov/treatie2.htm
This site provides links to the full text of several arms control treaties and agreements.

Status of Treaties

Many users are looking for information on the current status of a treaty and such
information is often difficult to find. Sometimes the only way to gather information
about a recent treaty is to phone either the U.S. Department of State Treaty Affairs Office
(202-647-2044) or the United Nations Treaty Section (212-963-3918). These phone
numbers are current as of 1999. Other possible resources to find out about the status of a
treaty include the following:

Congressional Index
This loose-leaf index, updated weekly, is an excellent source for finding the status of
current treaties pending before the U.S. Senate. It includes a status table for both old and
new treaties pending before the Senate.

Senate Treaty Document Series, 1982–
These documents are issued in a timelier manner than *TIAS* and may contain the text of
recent treaties. For a full description, see the entry above in "Full text resources for U.S.
treaties." It is indexed in *CIS Annual* ***.

UN Chronicle, 1975– (monthly)
This monthly publication by the United Nations may include recent treaty information. It
is indexed in *Readers' Guide to Periodical Literature* ***.

U.S. Department of State Dispatch, 1990– (monthly)
Formerly called the *Department of State Bulletin* (1939–1989) this monthly publication is
the main source for current U.S. treaty information. Information on the latest
developments to a treaty such as revisions and ratification are included. It is indexed in
Readers' Guide to Periodical Literature ***.

Hands on Exercises

It is important to follow up the three information sessions with some hands-on exercises.
The following list of questions can be used during or after the training session to help
participants use the resources they have been shown. The first two exercises, with all of
the steps, are included at the end of this chapter. All other exercises can be found on the
accompanying disk. Customize the exercises as needed for your individual library

situation.

- When was the Maastricht Treaty signed and when did it enter into force?
- What is the purpose of the Antarctic Treaty? Who were the signing parties? When was it signed and when did it come into force? What, if any, amendments were made to this treaty? Is it still in effect?
- What treaty ended Queen Anne's War? In what year? Who were the signing parties and what territories were granted to each party?
- Treaty of Non-Proliferation of Nuclear Weapons. How many articles are there in this treaty? When was it signed? When did it enter into force? Is it still in force? Find the full text.
- What percent of its territory was Mexico required to cede in the Treaty of Guadalupe Hidalgo? To which country was this land ceded?
- How many articles and annexes does the Treaty of Peace, signed by Jordan and Israel on 25 July 1994, contain? Find the full text of this treaty.
- What were the provisions placed on Germany by the Treaty of Versailles?
- When was the Treaty of Ghent signed?
- What treaty ended World War II?
- Who were the signing parties of the Treaty of Verdun?
- When did the Treaty of Paris enter into force?
- What is the Fort Laramie Treaty of 1868? Who were the signing parties?
- How many meals per day are required to be given to prisoners of war according to the Geneva Convention?
- What is the Treaty of Westphalia?
- Find the dates and signing parties for three nuclear arms reduction agreements, treaties, or conventions.
- Find the full text of the U.S. – Soviet INF Treaty.
- When was the Panama Canal Treaty signed? By what countries? Find the full text.
- What was the purpose of the Treaty of Peace between Turkey and the Balkans? When did it enter into force?
- What parties were involved in the Convention of Gastein? What year?

Treaties Exercise

When was the Maastricht Treaty signed and when did it enter into force?

Complete the steps listed below and briefly state the answer to the topic question.

Step 1   Locate a print resource.

Citation:

Step 2   Locate an electronic resource.

URL:

Step 3   Discuss the search strategy used in both steps 1 and 2.

Treaties Exercise

What is the purpose of the Antarctic Treaty? Who were the signing parties? When was it signed and when did it come into force? What, if any, amendments were made to this treaty? Is it still in effect?

Complete the steps listed below and briefly state the answer to the topic question.

Step 1   List the reference resources from this chapter that you think will best answer these questions.

Step 2   Explain why you chose these particular titles.

Step 3   Examine each title selected. What information was located in each title? Was the question fully answered?

Step 4   If your library does not own these titles, describe the search strategies you
         would use to find the answers with the available resources.

Step 5   If none of your in-house resources provide the answer, what search strategy
         would you use on the Internet?

Treaties Exercise

What treaty ended Queen Anne's War? In what year? Who were the signing parties?   What territories were granted to each party?

Complete the steps listed below and briefly state the answer to the topic question.

Step 1   List the titles from this chapter that you think will best answer these questions.

Step 2   Explain why you chose these particular titles.

Step 3   Examine each title selected. What information was located in each title? Was the question fully answered?

Step 4   If your library does not own these titles, describe the search strategies you would use to find the answers with the available resources.

Step 5   If none of your in-house resources provide the answer, what search strategy would you use on the Internet?

Notes:

BIBLIOGRAPHY RESOURCES

LAWRENCE L. TOMIKEL

Hillman Library Reference
UNIVERSITY OF PITTSBURGH

Introduction

The term "bibliography" is derived from the Greek word "bibliografia" and it literally means book writing. *The Random House Dictionary of the English Language* (1983) defines bibliography as

1) A complete or selective list of works compiled upon some common principle as authorship, subject, place of publication, or printer.
2) A list of source materials that are used or consulted in the preparation of a work or that are referred to in the text.
3) A branch of Library Science dealing with the history, physical description, comparison, and classification of books and other works.

There are countless other definitions of the word bibliography and those definitions have changed over time, but for the purposes of reference work, bibliographies are the base line which bring order out of chaos. They are the basic finding tools that we use to provide information to library users. Both information needs and library skills differ from patron to patron. The job of reference providers is to assist and instruct them to meet their information needs. Bibliographies provide one way of doing this.

Bibliographies are lists of existing resources. They tell us what material is available on a subject, person, or idea. They can also tell us what is not available and can be used to identify gaps in any field of research. They can help to answer basic reference queries where the user needs to begin looking for information. Bibliographies help users find information, whether it is a list of resources, verification of the existence of a resource, or completion of a partial citation.

Many library patrons ask reference department staff to help them verify the existence of a book, journal article, movie, recording, map, or other resource that they have either heard of or have used in the past and want to find. Patrons often ask the reference staff to fill in information that they need for a bibliography of their own. They may need the title, author, date, page numbers, or other things to complete citations of works used in their own research. Bibliographies provide one way to accomplish all of these.

Bibliographies are used in reference work to **FIND** and **VERIFY**. The exercises in this chapter are designed with these concepts in mind—to teach the reference provider to meet these basic information needs.

Objectives of the Instruction and Training

This chapter was designed to introduce the concepts of bibliographies to new reference providers. The instructions and exercises have been adapted to the use of bibliographies in daily reference work, emphasizing finding, creating, and verifying.

Types of Bibliographies

For the purposes of this instruction and training, the bibliographies have been grouped into the following categories:

- **catalogs,**
- **indexes and abstracts,**
- **subject specific sources,**
- **pathfinders,**
- **resources consulted and further reading, and**
- **the World Wide Web**

Most bibliographies fall into one or more of these categories and this list is hardly inclusive. Exercises will be built around each of these types to enable the trainees to evaluate, select, teach, and recommend resources to library patrons. The goal of reference service is to assist library users to find material to meet their information needs, and more importantly, to teach them to select and to use resources on their own.

Evaluation of Bibliographies

When selecting a bibliographic resource to meet user needs, you must consider the scope of the work. Does it meet the needs of the patron as determined by the reference interview with the patron? It is essential to ask the patron exactly what they are looking for when they ask you for information. Many times the library user will ask for one thing and want something totally different. For example, the patron may ask where the journals are, when, in reality, they need articles on a certain subject. They need an index, not just the location of the periodical collection.

Some points to consider when selecting a bibliography are:
Content: What subject matter does it cover?
Sciences, Arts, Humanities, Social Sciences, Statistics, etc.
Time: What time frame does it deal with?
Historical, Current, Both, or just certain time periods
Format: What types of material does it include?
Books, Articles, Manuscripts, Multimedia, Electronic Resources
Language: In what language or languages is it written?
Are the resources listed in more than one language?
Audience: What is the information level?
General, Subject Specific, Biased or unbiased?
Audience: Who are the intended users?
Professionals, General Public, Educational Attainment, Age

Authority: Who produced the resource?
   Subject Expert, Organization, For Profit Company
Availability: Where are the resources available?
   In House, Other Local Library, Nationwide, Internationally

The last point of availability is important. Does the patron just need or want items held in your library? How much information do they need? A few items or everything they can get? Do they have time for Interlibrary Loans or Document Delivery services? Again, this information will come from a successful reference interview with the library patron.

Finding Bibliographies

The best place to find bibliographies, and often the first one consulted, is the online catalog (OPAC) and/or the card catalog, both of which are bibliographies themselves.

When using Library of Congress subject headings, the term "bibliography" is both a subject heading and a sub-heading of other subject listings.

Bibliography—Bibliography
Baseball—Bibliography

When using the library's online catalog, remember to find out how your system treats punctuation marks and truncation. For example, in the NOTIS system, the double dashes between the subject heading and the sub-heading must be put in as shown. If your library still has a card catalog or partial card catalog, make a point of emphasizing the importance of finding older material or items that may not be on the electronic version.

When using keyword capabilities the term "bibliography" should be used in its singular form. That is the form used in LC subject headings and will retrieve more hits.

Keywords: Television and Bibliography

Searching in this manner will not only get you items with "bibliography" in the subject fields, but also items with that term in title fields and notes fields. You will find items that are themselves bibliographies, but also materials that contain bibliographies at the end of chapters or as supplements to the text.

Bibliographies are also found in the form of periodical indexes and abstracts both in print and electronic formats. These resources are often listed in library catalogs by title, subject, and keyword access.

Subject: Periodicals—Indexes
Keywords: Education and Indexes
Keywords: Education and Bibliography

Many libraries provide handouts and signage listing the titles and types of periodical indexes and their locations. If your library has them, include them as part of the materials for your instruction and training session.

Bibliographies are also created in-house in libraries and are designed to help users find information on certain subjects which are contained in that collection. Often these "pathfinder bibliographies" include "hot topics" currently popular, subjects in which the library has considerable collection strength, or are designed to answer frequently asked reference questions. They will list a wide variety of library resources that include information on the topic as well as library holdings that are primarily focused on the subject of the bibliography. They may include books, periodical indexes in both print and electronic formats, URLs of some relevant web pages, microforms, directories, maps, audio visual materials, appropriate organizations to contact, and other local resources. They should also include tips for searching both the library catalog and any relevant periodical indexes with examples of those searching tips.

These pathfinder bibliographies are often available as handouts either at or near the reference desk or other public service points. Many libraries are putting these bibliographies on their web pages, accessible through links from the Library Instruction home page or links from appropriate subject pages.

Bibliographies are also created and appended to published works to enable readers and researchers to know what resources the author or authors of those works consulted in their research. They can be found at the end of a book, chapter of a book, journal article, or encyclopedia entry. They also often list suggested further readings on the subject matter or topics related to it.

The World Wide Web is another resource to either create a bibliography of information or to find existing bibliographies that are published on web pages.

Types of Bibliographies

Catalogs
Catalogs are lists of materials with certain parameters or scope. They may be limited to items in specific collections, items currently available from publishers, items found in national libraries, items found in multiple collections, or items available from government information producing agencies. They are used to find existing bibliographies, create bibliographies to use in research, to verify the existence of a resource, and to complete partial citations to resources.

Online/Card Catalogs
Catalogs are often the first source consulted when seeking existing bibliographies or building a bibliography for research purposes. Trainees should have a solid foundation of title, author, subject, and keyword searching skills. They should also learn the value of any existing card catalogs and other finding aids in the library for finding older material or materials in non-traditional formats, such as audio visuals, microforms, and maps that are not included in the online catalog. The training instructor should point out that these items are held locally and should be readily available.

OCLC's *WorldCat* ***

OCLC (Online Computer Library Center) "is a nonprofit computer service and research organization whose network and services link more than 25,000 libraries in the U.S. and 63 countries and territories. OCLC services help libraries locate, acquire, catalog, access, and lend library materials." *WorldCat* is "the world's largest and most comprehensive bibliographic database."—*OCLC's web page.*

This immense database is used in reference services to locate and to verify materials held in libraries world wide. Trainees should be familiar with basic searching and many libraries have handouts on basic searching techniques.

National Union Catalog

The *NUC* is "a cumulative author list representing Library of Congress printed cards and titles reported by other American libraries."—*Pre-1956 Imprints of the NUC.* This multi-volume set is extremely useful to locate and verify items that may not be found in electronic catalogs such as OCLC because they may be old or rare. Access is mainly by author and will tell users not only that something exists, but which libraries own the item. This set does not contain many serial records. The *Union List of Serials* and *New Serial Titles* can be used to find and verify serial records.

Books in Print, 1948– ***

This is an author, subject, and title listing of books that are currently available and forthcoming from U.S. publishers and distributors of foreign publications as being available for purchase. The information included is compiled from listings sent in by publishers. If new books have not been reported, they are not listed. Many libraries provide the electronic version for their clientele. This source is valuable also for publisher addresses, telephone, fax, etc. Comparable resources are available for Canada, Britain, France, Germany, etc.

Bibliographic Index, 1938– ***

This index lists bibliographies published during the past year that have been issued either separately or as part of a journal article or a book. In order to be listed in this H.W. Wilson index, a bibliography must include at least 50 entries. The arrangement is by Library of Congress subject heading.

Monthly Catalog of United States Government Publications, 1895– ***

This is a listing of documents produced by various agencies in the U. S. government and is arranged in Superintendent of Documents classification order. This classification system might have to be explained to trainees if they have not had documents training sessions, a government publications reference course. Entries may be accessed by using author, title, subject, series/report, title keyword, and other indexes. It is available in print from the Government Printing Office as well as various electronic formats.

Indexes and Abstracts

Indexes and abstracts are bibliographic sources of periodical publications. Access to these resources is mainly by subject headings, though some also offer author and title access. Usually in the printed volumes there is subject cross referencing. In electronic formats, there is keyword capability as well as traditional subject searching done with thesauri. After the library catalog, these are the resources that are consulted when assisting library users in meeting their information needs. They offer more up-to-date information than book resources, but also are an excellent guide to finding primary source material for historical researching. It is essential to explain primary and secondary sources to the trainees. Many indexes and abstracts have both print and electronic formats. Show the trainees which ones are available in the library, what format they come in, where they are in the library, and explain the major subjects that they cover. Subject content and the time period covered are important considerations in selecting an index or abstract as a bibliographic tool.

Prepare a list of the indexes and abstracts that are held in your library that you can use in the finding and verifying exercises. You may want to pull older editions of the printed ones for your session and you should choose ones that are frequently used by your library patrons. See also the chapter that covers indexes and abstracts in Volume 1 of this title.

Subject Specific Bibliographies

These resources are what most people think of when they use the term "Bibliography." They are compilations of known materials on specific topics or people and their works. They usually provide full bibliographic citations to the materials giving titles, authors, publishers, dates, and pagination. Some are annotated and give a brief description of the content and scope of the resources that are included in the bibliography. These types of resources are mainly finding tools, they tell a user what is known. They may also be used to verify sources. They do have an additional use, that of narrowing or broadening a research topic. If the user is finding too much information on the topic, suggest a bibliography to narrow the focus. If you do not find sufficient sources, or any resources at all, suggest that the patron broaden the focus of the topic. Caution the trainees that printed and electronic bibliographies will contain items that are not available in the library and to pass that information on to patrons who are seeking their help.

Subject bibliographies are available for thousands and thousands of topics, subtopics, individuals, companies, etc. The bibliographies may be full-length books or they may simply be a short listing at the end of an article on the particular subject. The list that is included in this chapter is simply a sampling to show the variety which are available.

The Animal Rights Movement in the United States, 1975–1990. 1994.
The issues, philosophy, organizations, and activities of the animal rights movement are covered in this bibliography. The citations are divided by major animal rights issues, such as trapping and fur industry, circuses, zoos, animal experimentation, etc. There are author, title, and subject indexes.

Bibliography of Canadian Bibliographies = Bibliographie des bibliographies canadiennes. 1994 ed.

In this bibliography, Canadian is defined as information about Canada published anywhere, rather than just in Canada. Therefore, works published in Canada or of Canadian authorship which deal with a subject other than Canada and do not further studies of things, people, or events Canadian, have not been included.—*Introd.* The arrangement is by broad topic, year of publications, and then alphabetically by author. There are author, title and language indexes (English and French).

ELSI Bibliography: Ethical, Legal, & Social Implications of the Human Genome Project. 1994 ed.

This is a U.S. government publication from the Dept. of Energy (SuDocs E1.19:0591) which is kept up-to-date with supplements. Books, articles, and news articles from newspapers and science journals are cited. It is available in print or on microfiche.

Essential Shakespeare: An Annotated Bibliography of Major Modern Studies. 1993 ed.

This bibliography includes an annotated listing of the most important criticism on Shakespeare in the twentieth century through 1991, according to the editor. The arrangement is categorized under: General Studies; The Poems and Sonnets; The English-History Plays, The Comedies; The Tragedies; and The Romances. Under each work, the bibliography is arranged by reference works, editions, textual studies, criticism, and stage history. Users may also consult *World Shakespeare Bibliography* on CD-ROM.

Notable Women in World History: A Guide to Recommended Biographies and Autobiographies. 1998.

The author lists four main criteria for inclusion in the collection: that a woman must have been born outside the United States, that she must have made a noteworthy achievement, that a full-length biography be available which was published since 1970, and that the biography be listed in the Library of Congress catalog. One appendix lists the notable women by date of birth, another by country of birth, and a third by title, occupation, or main area of interest. There is also an alphabetical index of names.

Pathfinders

Pathfinder bibliographies are used to guide and instruct a library user. They are usually subject specific and library specific. Many are generated in-house and will tell patrons what resources are in the library collection or in local libraries on specific topics. Often the subject covered is either a "hot topic," a frequently asked question, or deals with a particular strength of the collection. Pathfinders are found usually in the form of printed handouts displayed in the reference area or at the reference desk, but they also can be found through links on the library's home page.

Pathfinder bibliographies will list relevant encyclopedias and dictionaries, indexes and abstracts, journals, statistical sources, government publications, audio visual materials, web sites and links, associations and organizations, electronic resources, bibliographies, and other materials held locally. They also include tips on searching the OPAC or card catalog. They provide relevant subject headings and key words for searching indexes and abstracts in both print and electronic formats and many include information to help the user find the items in the library.

The Library Orientation Exchange (LOEX) at the Michigan State University, Ypsilanti, collects pathfinders from its members. If your library is a member of LOEX, you may request to borrow a variety of pathfinders for ideas. One pathfinder developed at the University of Pittsburgh on finding company information is included on the accompanying disk; call numbers and most library-specific information have been stripped. You may modify the pathfinder in any way for your own library use.

Resources Consulted and Further Readings

Resources consulted bibliographies are a listing of the materials that an author has used in doing research to produce a body of work. They are found at the end of books, chapters in books, journal articles, encyclopedia entries, and research papers. These listings are excellent sources of specific information and can be used to both broaden a research topic or narrow the focus of a body of research.

Further reading bibliographies are also found at the end of bodies of work. They are usually not items that were used to produce a body of work, but they do give readers a means of expanding their knowledge of the topic discussed. They are particularly useful at the end of introductory materials such as encyclopedia articles. Remind the trainees of the value of encyclopedic entries as a means of introducing researchers to topics that may be unfamiliar to them. They may refer patrons to general encyclopedias such as the *Britannica* *** or the *Americana* *** or to more subject specific ones such as the *Encyclopedia of Philosophy* or the *McGraw-Hill Encyclopedia of Science & Technology*.

Another very informative introductory source to which I refer library patrons is the *CQ Researcher*. This is a weekly publication with annual cumulations and indexes. Each issue covers one "hot topic" or one currently controversial issue. It provides information on the "issues," "background," "current situation," "outlook," and "more information" on the topic covered as well as "sidebar and graphics" type of information. As a bibliographic tool the "more information" category lists a bibliography of selected sources used and a next step listing of additional articles from current periodicals. There is also a selected list of organizations and associations to contact for more information.

The World Wide Web

The World Wide Web is a constantly growing, multi-level electronic resource of information on just about any topic that is produced by just about any person or organization. Caution the trainees that when using the Web as a resource they should evaluate the sites they refer to patrons. Who produced the site? Was it an educational organization, government agency, company, association, or private citizen? Does the producer have a bias? Is the site relevant for the research topic? Are there useful links provided? Are there accurate and useful up-to-date statistics?

Using the web as a finding tool for bibliographies greatly expands the library's resources and potentials. One can connect to a multitude of other online library catalogs, electronic periodical indexes, some with full text articles, government documents, association and organization home pages, as well as subject bibliographies that have already been created and posted on the web. A useful search strategy on a web searching service is to enter the subject keywords and bibliographies. For example: "Bibliographies and Civil War" or "Bibliographies and Astronomy." Many of these bibliographies found on the web will give current as well as historical sources of information.

The web can also be used as a verifying tool in reference work. One can connect to other library catalogs and periodical indexes to provide information to fill in incomplete citations. Searching on electronic resources that have key word capabilities is immensely easier when all that is known is the author's last name, the subject area or the work, and maybe part of the title and a guess at the date. Connecting to online full text newspapers sites is a good way of finding and verifying information queries from library users. Many times I have had patrons come to the reference desk and say "I remember reading an article in the paper some months ago on ...." Both local and national newspapers can be found on the web by just using the name of the paper as the key words in a search.

Style Manuals

Often students and researchers will come to the reference desk and request help in creating bibliographies to append to their body of work. This is another aspect of bibliographies in reference work. Publishers and professors will ask that works cited in bibliographies adhere to standards so that all monographs, chapters from books, journal articles, web sites, etc., will be in the same format. This makes it easier for the user of the bibliography to know where to find the cited work. Below is a list of some of the more frequently used style manuals that will explain and give examples of how to cite different types of sources in bibliographies. You may want to have one or two of these on hand to show to the trainees.

> *Publication Manual of the American Psychological Association (APA)*
> *MLA Handbook*
> Turabian's *A Manual for Writers of Term Papers, Theses, and Dissertations*
> *Chicago Manual of Style*
> *Electronic Style: A Guide to Citing Electronic Information*

Hands-on Exercises

There are six very unique exercises in this chapter and the instructions are explained in detail. They have also been set up on worksheets in the text and they are also included on the accompanying disk. Any of the exercises may be customized to fit the circumstances in individual libraries.

Exercise 1: Finding Subject Specific Bibliographies in Catalogs

- This exercise should be done in teams of two or three trainees.
- Using the local catalog, the instructing librarian should find 4 book-length bibliographies on a very broad topic. Some sample topics could be Sports, American Literature, Indians of North America, or Gerontology. Assign the same topic to each team, if the class is large, so that the results can be compared. Make sure the library collection has ample titles available on the topic you choose.
- Have the trainees search the catalog to select titles and pull the books from the shelves.
- Each team will then evaluate its choices according to the criteria listed below. A criteria sheet is listed at the end of this chapter and may be used for duplication. Duplicate choices will be shared, but evaluations should not be shared until all teams are finished.
    1. Subject coverage
    2. Time frames
    3. Types of material included
    4. Languages included
    5. Information content
    6. Intended users
    7. Producer of bibliography
    8. Availability

Exercise 2: Finding Subject Specific Book Length Bibliographies Not Held Locally

- This exercise may be used as a follow-up to exercise no. 1; use the same teams if it is treated as a follow-up.
- Trainees are to find 6 more potential book length bibliographies on the same topic as in Exercise 1 using *Books in Print*, *OCLC*, *WorldCat*, and/or the World Wide Web. At least 2 sources should be from the Web.
- Have the teams evaluate their choices as best as they can without actually having the item in hand.
- They can check for local holdings of their choices, but that is not necessary.
- The choices are to be discussed as in Exercise 1.

Exercise 3: Creating Subject Specific Bibliographies

- This exercise can be done either in teams or individually.
- Using the catalog and locally held indexes and abstracts, the trainees must create a list of resources on the same topic as in the above exercises. This will be list of 5 to 7 books on the subject, not bibliographies, and about 8 journal articles. The book resources must include at least one dictionary and one encyclopedia. Four articles are to be selected using electronic indexes and four using print indexes.
- The trainees are to annotate this bibliography with a sentence or two describing the works chosen as well as the reason they were chosen.

Exercise 4: Verifying Citations Using Catalogs, Indexes, and Abstracts

- This exercise is planned as a team exercise.
- Verifying and filling in incomplete citations is a constant service in reference work. It can be both rewarding as in "Yes, I did it." and frustrating as in "I need more information!" Point out to the trainees that this part of reference work will tax their detective skills. They must think about which resources to use to answer the reference question—often with only a few clues. Tell them that a proper and thorough interview with the patron will often be necessary. Try to elicit as much data about the citation as possible. Many times the information the librarian is given is second hand or it may be something the patron once used but did not get all the needed bibliographic information to find the item again or to cite it. As in actual reference work at the desk, these kinds of questions are not usually answered alone; many times more than one librarian will work on the question.

  Hints: Check for variant spellings of names, use synonyms for key words and subjects, check out the date of publication if possible, use multiple databases in related fields, and use printed resources. Try to determine if the item is a book, a journal article, a chapter from a book, conference proceedings, or what? Chapters from books and conference proceedings are not easy to find or verify. This exercise will not cover them in order to allow the trainees time to develop some basic skills on which they can build.

- The instructing librarian is to create a list of 10 incomplete citations. Five are to be monographs held in your library or accessible through OCLC, BIP, etc., and five are to be journal citations that can be found in print or electronic indexes and abstracts that are in your collection. Note: Don't be too obscure since this is a training session designed to develop basic skills.
- Phrase the citations in the form of a reference question from a library patron and give them enough information to establish the subject matter or kind of material, i.e., book or journal article.

Examples 1: "I used an article about Title IX and its progress from the Department of Education. I don't have the exact title, but it was fairly recent. Can you help me relocate it? I need it for my bibliography."

> Answer: The item is actually an *ERIC* document "Title IX: 25 years of progress," 1997.

Example 2: "My professor told me to read a recent article by Bradley on science education and women. She said it's in the library. Where is it?"

> Answer: Science Education for a Minority within a Minority. by Rosa M. Bradley, *American Biology Teacher* v. 59 n2 p73–79 Feb. 1997.

Examples 1 and 2 can be found using *ERIC* in electronic form and using keyword searching.

Example 3: "I heard about two new exciting books on camping. One is about the Lewis and Clark trail and the other is about the Smoky Mountains and was written by Malloy. Do you have them or where can I buy them?

Answer: Two questions in one. First book is *Following the Lewis & Clark Trail – A Vacation Guide for Campers*." Warner, Doten, 1998. Second book is *Best in Tent Camping – Smoky Mountains*." Molloy, Jimmy, 1997.

Example 3 can be found in *Books in Print* or perhaps in your library catalog. Note that the patron spelled one author as **Malloy**, but the correct spelling is **Molloy**.

Example 4: "I read an article in *Science News* a while ago about dinosaurs and birds. Could you help me find it again? I want to use it for my term paper."

Answer: "A fowl flight: fossil finds recharge debate about birds and dinosaurs." Richard Monastersky. *Science News* August 23, 1997 v152 n8 p120.

Example 5: "I've never been here before, but my friend told me about a really good review of a book by Norman on horned dinosaurs. He said he found it here. Where is it?"

Answer: "Journey round the horns." (review of book on horned dinosaurs) David A. Norman. *New Scientist* Dec 14, 1996 v152 n2060 p44.

Examples 4 and 5 can be answered using the *Expanded Academic ASAP* using keyword searching. Note that in the second question the author's name Norman could be a first or a last name.

Note: Example 1 has been set up as an exercise. You may substitute other verification questions for the other trainees in the class. The examples shown above can be used, however, many others can be gleaned from actual questions at the reference desk or from your own experiences. This exercise should be done after the instruction session and the trainer should be available to give hints and direction since there is no real dialog with an actual patron.

Exercise 5: Finding "Resources Consulted" and "Further Readings"

- This is a short individual exercise.
- The instructing librarian should give each trainee a broad topic. They are to use two different encyclopedias and locate the same topic in each.
- Trainees are to compare and contrast the bibliographies at the end of each article and answer the following questions:
  Which is more inclusive?
  Which is more useful to a researcher new to the subject matter?
  Are any of the citations the same?
  Do they give full bibliographic citations or incomplete citations?

Exercise 6: Creating a Pathfinder Bibliography

- This exercise is planned for an individual trainee who will work on a unique topic. The purpose of the exercise is to create a subject bibliography specific to a library. The chosen topic must fit the strengths of the library collection, cover a "hot topic," or would help patrons researching a frequently asked question. The handout in this chapter, "Finding Company Information," is an example of a pathfinder bibliography.

- The pathfinder should list relevant books, encyclopedias, dictionaries, indexes and abstracts, journals and newspapers, statistical sources, web sites, associations, almanacs, handbooks, bibliographies, and or other resources held in the library. It states the scope of the pathfinder and any relevant time frame. It should also include call numbers and locations in the local library. Examples of keywords and searching hints for electronic resources should be included.

- The pathfinder should not be longer than 3 to 4 pages and should include the date on which it was created.

- Discuss the need to update pathfinders periodically. They should conform to a style used in the library. For the purposes of this exercise, it may be submitted on disk. Pathfinders are a very practical addition to reference service; this exercise provides a useful contribution to the reference department.

Exercise—Bibliographies

Finding Subject Specific Bibliographies in Catalogs

Your team has been assigned a topic. Complete the exercise according to these steps. First, review the complete exercise.

Step 1   Search your library catalog for four full-length bibliographies on this topic.

Document your search strategy.

Step 2   List the titles you select.

Pull the titles from the bookshelves.

Step 3   Evaluate the titles according to the following criteria.

Use a separate evaluation handout for each title.

1. Subject coverage
2. Time frames
3. Types of material included
4. Languages included
5. Information content
6. Intended users
7. Producer of bibliography
8. Availability

Step 4   Select five titles from each bibliography.

          List the titles on your evaluation sheet.

Step 5   Search the library catalog to see if they are held by the library.

Step 6   Titles that are not held by your library must be searched in OCLC, *WorldCat*,
          NUC, or any other networked resource to determine a holding library.

Step 7   Be prepared to discuss your reasons for choosing the four book-length
          bibliographies with the rest of the class.

Exercise—Bibliographies

Finding Subject Specific Book Length Bibliographies That Are Not Held Locally

Your team has been assigned a topic. Complete the exercise according to these steps. First, review the complete exercise.

Step 1   Find six (6) book length bibliographies using *Books in Print, OCLC, WorldCat,* and/or the World Wide Web.

Step 2   List the titles you select and the source from which they were obtained. Note: two sources are to be from the WWW.

Step 3   Evaluate the titles according to the following criteria.

Use a separate evaluation handout for each title.

1. Subject coverage
2. Time frames
3. Types of material included
4. Languages included
5. Information content
6. Intended users
7. Producer of bibliography
8. Availability

Step 4   Check your catalog for local holdings.

Step 5   Be prepared to discuss your reasons for choosing the six book-length
          bibliographies with the rest of the class.

Exercise—Bibliographies

Creating Subject Specific Bibliographies

Your team has been assigned a topic. Complete the exercise according to these steps. First, review the complete exercise.

Step 1   Use your library catalog to create a list of resources on the your assigned topic. The list is to include **five to seven books** (not bibliographies).

Include one topic dictionary and one topic encyclopedia in the book selections.

List your book resources.

Step 2   Your list is to include **eight journal articles**.

Locate **four of the articles** using electronic indexes. List the articles.

Locate **four of the articles** using print indexes or abstracts.

Step 3   Annotate this bibliography with a sentence or two describing the works chosen.
          Note also why a work was chosen.

Exercise—Bibliographies

Verifying Citations Using catalogs, Indexes, and Abstracts

Questions from two patrons are listed below. Explain your search strategy to find the information the patron needs.

Step 1   A patron came to the reference desk and said,

"I heard about two new exciting books on camping. One is about the Lewis and Clark trail and the other is about the Smoky Mountains and was written by Malloy. Do you have them or where can I buy them?"

Step 2   What would you do to help this patron?

Document your search strategy and list the resources you used.

Exercise—Bibliographies

Finding "Resources Consulted" and "Further Readings"

You have been given a broad topic. Complete the exercise according to these steps. First, review the complete exercise.

Step 1   Select two different encyclopedias. List those you select.

Step 2   Find the entries for your topic in each set.

Step 3   Compare and contrast the bibliographies at the end of each article by answering the following questions:

Which is more inclusive? Explain your reasons.

Which is more useful to a research new to the subject matter? Explain your reasons.

Are any of the citations the same?

Do they give full citations or incomplete citations?

Exercise—Bibliographies

Creating a Pathfinder Bibliography

You may select your own topic for the pathfinder, but choose a topic that fits the strengths of your library collection, that covers a "hot topic," or would help patrons.

Step 1   Choose a topic and discuss its appropriateness with the instructor.

         List your topic.

Step 2   Examine the example included in this chapter: Finding Company Information.

Step 3   Create a bibliography of your topic specific to the holdings of your library.

         The pathfinder should list relevant books, encyclopedias, dictionaries, indexes and abstracts, journal and newspaper titles, statistical source, web sites, associations, almanacs, handbooks, bibliographies, and/or other resources held in your library.

         The pathfinder should include information as to the scope and any relevant time frames.

         It should also include call numbers and locations. (All location and call number information has been eliminated from the example in this chapter.)

         Provide keywords, subject headings and searching hints, especially for electronic resources. Some examples would be useful to the user.

         The pathfinder should be three to four pages in length. It should include the date on which it was completed.

COMPANY RESOURCES;
AN ANNOTATED BIBLIOGRAPHY

SCOPE

This bibliography is a listing of sources found in the Hillman Library. It is designed for researchers seeking information about particular companies and not about specific industries. Some of the resources, such as those in electronic formats, will include both types of information.

Additional resources may be found at Pitt's Business Library, 138 Mervis Hall (648-1669); at the Carnegie Public Library's downtown Business Information Center (281-4663); and at the Carnegie Public Library's Job and Career Education Center at the Main Branch in Oakland (621-3133).

Resources in Electronic Format

Pittcat Plus Resources
See the separate Pittcat Plus series of handouts for each of these products for more information.

ABI/Inform is an index to articles in business from over 800 periodicals covering 1988 to the present.

> Search by keyword: k=alcoa
>
> k=alcoa.co. (the **.co.** makes the computer search only for alcoa as a company name)

Periodical Abstracts is an index to articles from over 1,650 academic, popular, and business periodicals in the U.S., covering 1989 to the present.

> Search by keyword: k=pepsi
>
> Note: Full-text of articles with a "*ProQuest* #" are available at the *ProQuest* printing station, located near the Information Desk on the ground floor. See the *ProQuest* printing handout for more details.

CD-NET Resources
Some, but not all of these titles have separate handouts.

CD Newsbank contains recent full-text articles from newspapers and wire services covering topics of national and international importance.

> Search by company name.

Computer Select contains over 12,000 documents on computer companies.

> Select "Computer Company Profiles" from the menu, and search by company name.

F&S Index Plus Text is an index to abstracts, excerpts, and selected full-text of articles from over 1,000 business sources covering 1990 to the present.

> To retrieve records containing information on a specific company, use the company name field. Press <F5>, and enter the first part of the company name.

Stand-alone CD-ROM Resources

New York Times Ondisc contains the full editorial content of the *New York Times* from 1991 to the present. Earlier years are covered by the printed *New York Times Index*, located on Index Carrel #15 on the ground floor of Hillman.
 Search by company name.

Online Services

Persons affiliated with the University of Pittsburgh are entitled to varying amounts of subsidized online searching on a wide range of databases. Fees will be charged to those not affiliated with the University. Stop by the Reference Consulting Center in room G-7 Hillman (next to the Information Desk) during business hours for more information.

RESOURCES IN PRINTED FORMAT

Note: The informational content will vary from source to source.

National Directories and Sources

Business Periodicals Index
A printed index to articles in English language business periodicals.

Business Rankings Annual
Worldwide ranking of companies, products, services, and activities by subject.

Career Guide
Contains locational, descriptive, and employment information.

Directory of Foreign Manufactures in the United States
Contains locational, descriptive, and parent company information.

Dun's Business Rankings
Public and private business ranked with industry category and state.

Dun's Consultants Directory
Contains locational, descriptive, statistical, and personnel information.

High Technology Market Place Directory
Contains locational, descriptive, statistical, and personnel information.

Hoover's Handbook of American Business
Contains in-depth locational, descriptive, statistical, personnel, and historical information.

How to Find Information About Companies

Features published sources, databases and CD-ROMs, federal, state, and local documents, company watchers, industry participants, research services, etc.

Job Seeker's Guide
Contains locational, descriptive, statistical, personnel, and employment information.

Million Dollar Directory
Contains locational, descriptive, statistical, and personnel information on America's leading public and private companies.

Phonefiche
Telephone directories on microfiche for U.S. communities with populations over 500,000. Includes both white and yellow page directories.

Regional Directory of Minority and Women-Owned Business Firms
Contains locational, descriptive, statistical, and personnel information.

Standard and Poor's Register of Corporations
Contains locational, descriptive, statistical, and personnel information.

Standard Directory of Advertising Agencies
Contains locational, descriptive, statistical, and personnel information as well as branch offices and a list of accounts.

Thomas Register of American Manufacturers
Contains locational and descriptive information, as well as "yellow page" type ads and company profiles.

Local Directories and Sources

Dun's Regional Business Directory (Pittsburgh area only)
Contains locational and descriptive information.

The Industrial Directory: Manufacturing Plants in Allegheny County
Contains locational, descriptive, and statistical information.

Major Firms in the Pittsburgh Metropolitan Area
Contains locational, descriptive, statistical, and personnel information.

Minority, Women-Owned Business Directory
Contains locational, descriptive, and personnel information.

Pennsylvania Industrial Directory
Contains locational, descriptive, statistical, and personnel information.

Pennsylvania Technology Directory
Contains locational, descriptive, statistical, and personnel information.

Women Directory: A Directory of Women-Owned Businesses
Contains locational, descriptive, and personnel information.

Local Telephone Directories

Bell Atlantic Business to Business Yellow Pages for the Greater Pittsburgh and Suburban Area

The Donnelley Directory for Pittsburgh and Allegheny County

Greater Pittsburgh Black Business Directory
Contains yellow pages-type information.

Greater Pittsburgh White Pages

Greater Pittsburgh Yellow Pages

Local Newspaper Articles

Pittsburgh Post-Gazette (for the years 1989–present)
Pittsburgh Business Times
These sources may be searched through the Dialog Database System. Persons affiliated with the University of Pittsburgh are entitled to varying amounts of subsidized searches. Fees will be charged to those not affiliated with the University.

New Pittsburgh Courier
This nationally known newspaper can be searched on the CD-NET in the *Ethnic Newswatch* database.

Local Historical Company Information

The Archives of Industrial Society
The AIS is a collection of historical records of Pittsburgh and Western Pennsylvania industries, organization, and institutions.

Larry L. Tomikel 7/96

Criteria for Evaluating Bibliographies

Title:

Subject coverage:

Time frames:

Types of material included:

Languages included:

Information content:

Intended users:

Producer of bibliography:

Availability:

Notes:

Notes: